Kosher Calm

Meditation & Self-Help Tools
For Health & Healing

Inspired by the Teachings of
Rabbi Menachem M. Schneerson
The Lubavitcher Rebbe

Rabbi Aryeh Siegel

McNae, Marlin & Mackenzie
Book and Periodical Publishers

Copyright © 2025 by McNae, Marlin and MacKenzie Publishers, Ltd., all rights reserved. Printed in the United States of America and in the United Kingdom. Let it be known that copyright shall be protected and defended against infringement by the Publisher.

Except as permitted by the United States Copyright Act of 1976, and the UK Copyright, Designs and Patents Act of 1988, no part of this publication may be reproduced, stored in a retrieval system or transmitted, in any form or by any means, electronic, mechanical, photocopying, recording, or otherwise without the prior written permission of the Author or the Publisher.

www.m3publishers.com

ISBN-979-8-89940-254-8

Front Cover Design by: KrinskyDesign.com
Editing: Sally Boyles, Lucy Spencer, Jerry Freeman, Doyle L. Perkins

Books by Rabbi Aryeh Siegel

Transcendental Deception: Behind the TM curtain –
bogus science, hidden agendas, and David Lynch's campaign to push a million public school kids into Transcendental Meditation

Please contact the Author at
rabbiaryeh@koshermeditation.com

http://koshercalm.org/

"In the mid-1970s, as leading rabbis issued strong prohibitions against Eastern meditation, the Rebbe took a revolutionary stance—calling on medical professionals to develop kosher alternatives for managing stress. Answering the Rebbe's passionate appeal, "Kosher Calm" unlocks his pioneering vision. In an era of extreme anxiety and global upheaval, it provides essential tools for finding peace within while staying true to tradition."

- Rabbi Mendel Kalmenson

"Reb Aryeh Siegel has heeded the Rebbe's fervent call from years past and crafted a profound book to alleviate the burdens of stress. The Rebbe, in a passionate public address and in countless letters, implored medical professionals to devise effective Kosher meditation practices for stress relief, thus nurturing healthier and more balanced lives. This book embodies that vision, bringing tranquility and harmony. Yashar Koach."

- Rabbi Dov Ber Pinson

"In my twenty years as a medical psychologist specializing in trauma and grief, one truth stands clear: healing must align with who we are and what we believe. This understanding became even more vital in my work with ZAKA volunteers, who regularly face scenes most of us cannot imagine.

When I first encountered Kosher Calm, I was struck by how seamlessly it merged meditation with science while maintaining deep respect for Jewish tradition. Research consistently shows that regular meditation triggers a relaxation response, reducing stress and building resilience. For our ZAKA volunteers, who confront trauma almost daily, we needed a meditation program that understood them, spoke their language, and honored their values. Kosher Calm delivers exactly that.

The program's meditation animations, presented in Hebrew and English, effectively complement the written guidance. While meditation isn't a cure-all, these techniques have earned their place in our therapeutic toolkit."

- Dr. Vered Atzmon Mushulam
  Head of ZAKA's Resilience Division

"As a psychiatrist, I wholeheartedly endorse *Kosher Calm*. Rabbi Aryeh Siegel adeptly presents evidence-based self-help tools for managing stress and enhancing emotional well-being consistent with Jewish law and tradition. Rabbi Siegel doesn't merely instruct us to relax—he shows us how. With step-by-step guidance, he teaches us how to elicit the relaxation response, our nervous system's natural antidote to the often-overused fight-or-flight response. Additionally, he examines the significance of belief and cognitive restructuring in attaining mental balance, skillfully intertwining the wisdom of the Lubavitcher Rebbe with contemporary findings in stress management."

- Miriam Grossman, MD, Child, Adolescent, and Adult Board-Certified Psychiatrist

"As a Rabbi who has witnessed thousands of Jewish travelers seeking spirituality in India over the past twenty-five years, I cannot recommend "Kosher Calm" highly enough. Too many young people turn to Eastern practices when seeking inner peace. "Kosher Calm" provides a powerful alternative, an easy-to-learn technique for managing stress and anxiety without religious or philosophical overlays. Because it works at any level of observance, it is an invaluable resource for Jews worldwide."

- Rabbi Dror Shaul, Dharamsala, India:

"Kosher Calm is a rare book that fulfills its promise to disentangle meditation from religion. Rabbi Siegel speaks with authority stemming from decades of in-depth experience with Hindu Transcendental Meditation (TM) and orthodox Judaism. Siegel documents how promoters of TM and Mindfulness-Based Stress Reduction (MBSR), eager for institutional funding and legitimacy, have misled the unwary—notably public school children—into participating in Hindu and Buddhist religious practices without giving them an informed choice to do so. Siegel does not merely denounce but also offers an alternative. Kosher Calm presents a meditation practice that Jewish people and practitioners of other or no religious faiths might find kosher."

- Candy Gunther Brown, Ph.D. Professor of Religious Studies, Indiana University

Why I Wrote This Book:
My Journey to Kosher Meditation

In 2015, I read a biography of Rabbi Menachem Schneerson (1902–1994), the Lubavitcher Rebbe. (Throughout this book, I will refer to him as the Rebbe.) Reading this biography transformed my understanding of my life's journey. At 71, I was a Los Angeles real estate broker who had helped establish two Chabad synagogues and a thriving Jewish elementary school with over 350 students. But there was a pivotal chapter of my life that, for decades, I kept mainly to myself.

In the mid-1970s, I trained with Maharishi Mahesh Yogi to become a Transcendental Meditation (TM) teacher. My wife and I spent ten years immersed in meditation, yoga, and Hindu scripture—four hours daily until 1981. We both worked as top executives in the TM national organization. These experiences and my extensive academic background in public health planning and behavioral science research seemed irrelevant to my eventual career in real estate and as a chossid of the Rebbe.

I first met the Rebbe in 1978 on Rosh Chodesh outside Chabad's headquarters in Brooklyn, New York. He wished me "a good month." This three-second encounter would prove more significant than I could have ever imagined. At the time, my wife and I maintained our four-hour meditation practice while being completely observant Jews—an unusual combination.

Only decades later did I learn that six months before our encounter, the Rebbe had issued a confidential memorandum to an estimated 50 mental health professionals. In it, he identified Transcendental Meditation as the most dangerous of all Eastern meditations for exposing tens of thousands of Jewish youth and adults to idolatry and trapping many in cults.

The Rebbe's approach to Eastern practices in 1977 was remarkably nuanced. While other Jewish leaders rushed to condemn meditation outright, he saw what they missed: beneath the religious trappings were valuable techniques for reducing stress and improving mental health. Instead of issuing a blanket prohibition like his contemporaries, he distinguished between meditation's religious elements and the method itself, which wasn't inherently religious—it was simply a tool that research documented had proven effective in reducing stress and anxiety.

This insight is more relevant today than ever. Three out of four American adults battle stress-related symptoms daily, while in Israel, more than half of the adult Jewish population struggles with clinical levels of anxiety. Fortunately, our bodies come equipped with a natural antidote: the relaxation response, our built-in defense against stress. Meditation is a profoundly effective method for eliciting this response. The challenge has been accessing this response while remaining in sync with Jewish values.

In the strongest possible language, the Rebbe implored mental health experts versed in Jewish law to develop protocols for kosher meditation. Unfortunately, these protocols were never developed, and the basic technique he sought seemingly eluded him.

Kosher Calm answers this call. With the support of an animated guide (in both English and Hebrew) and using a focus word of your own choice, you will learn a straightforward, simple meditation technique. Each chapter builds upon the last, offering proven tools for stress management and building emotional resilience. This isn't a book of mysticism or new-age philosophy; it's a practical guide for better living, grounded in research and Jewish law.

In these pages, you'll discover a meditation accessible to everyone, regardless of background or experience level. Through progressive chapters, you'll learn how to quiet your mind, reduce stress, and enhance your focus—all while maintaining complete alignment with Torah principles. The goal is to enable you to develop a sustainable meditation practice that fits seamlessly into your Jewish life.

The meditation practice introduced here is simple yet powerful. It allows your mind to naturally find its quiet center and automatically elicit the relaxation response, our built-in antidote to stress overload. Whether facing daily pressures, anxiety, or seeking balance, this book offers a path forward. This is more than a meditation guide; it's a roadmap to finding peace in our chaotic world while staying true to Torah values.

It took me over 40 years to understand why I became a meditation teacher and studied health planning and behavioral science research. What once seemed like divergent paths—being a TM teacher, an Orthodox Jew, and a behavioral scientist—were stepping stones that led to this moment. Each experience was essential preparation for writing this book. I am incredibly grateful to my wife, Tova Hinda, for initiating our journey to the Rebbe and providing extraordinary fulfillment in my life. My heart is full of gratitude to the Rebbe, who has guided our family for almost 50 years and given meaning to life experiences I didn't understand until now. This book is my attempt to honor his vision.

Welcome to your journey toward inner peace—the kosher way. Let's begin.

Rabbi Aryeh Siegel

Table of Contents

Introduction 1

Chapter 1: The Lubavitcher Rebbe's Vision for Therapeutic Kosher Meditation... 7

Chapter 2: The Impact of Stress on Health and Well-Being 15

Chapter 3: The Relaxation Response: Harnessing the Power of the Mind 19

Chapter 4: The Rebbe's Meditation Guidelines 31

Chapter 5: Preparing to Meditate 41

Chapter 6: Your First Meditation..................................... 47

Chapter 7: Questions and Answers for New Meditators.. 51

Chapter 8: If Meditation Gets Bumpy: Managing Resistance, Restlessness, Discomfort, and Trauma 61

Chapter 9: The Critical Role of Belief in Healing 75

Chapter 10: Cognitive Restructuring, Reframing, and Positivity... 83

Chapter 11: Resilience: How to Bounce Back Better 101

Chapter 12: Mind–Body Techniques May Help Certain Health Conditions 107

Chapter 13: Non-Kosher Practices 119

Chapter 14: Yoga 127

Chapter 15: Mantra Meditations 147

Chapter 16: Mindfulness and Mindfulness-Based Stress Release 157

Chapter 17: The Power That Made the Body Heals the Body 165

A Message to Healthcare Providers 169

Appendix A: Letters from the Rebbe on Meditation 173

Appendix B: Information for Healthcare Providers 229

Glossary 233

Notes 239

Bibliography 255

בס"ד

**The Power That Made the Body
Heals the Body**

It Happens No Other Way

Introduction

Kosher Meditation for Health and Healing

Finding inner peace is more important than ever in today's world. Stress has become a constant companion, impacting our physical health, emotional well-being, and overall quality of life. Yet within our bodies lies a natural antidote: the relaxation response, our intrinsic mechanism for combating stress. This self-help book, inspired by the teachings of the Lubavitcher Rebbe, Rabbi Menachem Mendel Schneerson, offers a practical approach to stress management through meditation that aligns with Jewish law and tradition.

The Rebbe recognized a crucial need: Jews require effective, scientifically sound methods to cope with life's mounting pressures. His interest wasn't in developing mystical or spiritually oriented meditation practices but in establishing a practical kosher approach to stress reduction—one that could help people lead healthier, more balanced lives.

This book presents a simple, scientifically validated technique for activating the relaxation response. The method is easy to learn and is designed to help you manage daily tensions and enhance overall well-being while adhering to Jewish law. At its core is a nondirective meditation technique that utilizes a focus word of your choice. This approach is gentle and effortless, allowing the focus word to naturally guide your attention to quieter levels of the mind. The meditation takes just minutes to learn, opening the door to a lifetime of inner peace.

Animation

For visual learners, a fifteen-minute English and Hebrew animation titled "Learning How to Do Kosher Meditation" complements the written instructions in Chapter 4, "Meditation Guidelines and Preparing to Meditate."

In this step-by-step animation, you will learn:

- A straightforward and effective method for activating your body's natural relaxation response.
- How to prepare for meditation
- Selecting a focus word
- Understanding the role of thoughts in meditation

Viewing tip: Watch the animation twice—first to understand what to expect and how to prepare, and then again when you're ready to practice. This two-step method will help you gain the most benefit from the animation. You can also pause the animation at any time to make the suggested arrangements. You might want to speed through the five-minute hourglass timer during the first viewing.

Animation links are available on both Vimeo and YouTube. If you experience difficulty accessing these URLs in your browser, the animations can also be found at KosherCalm.org

English Version:
Vimeo:
https://vimeo.com/1070922680/7810c893be?share=copy
YouTube: https://youtu.be/V6NaToT6IqI

Hebrew Version:
Vimeo:
https://vimeo.com/1071511040/338bf950ca?share=copy
YouTube: https://youtu.be/2kYaDVElqro

The Need for Meditation Today

The global mental health crisis has reached unprecedented levels. In 2022, the American Psychological Association found that over three-quarters of adults in the United States experienced stress symptoms, including headaches, fatigue, and depression.[1]

Israel is grappling with particularly acute challenges. At the peak of the second wave (October 2020) of COVID-19, 29% of Israelis reported experiencing extreme or highly extreme anxiety symptoms.[2] The situation worsened dramatically after the October 7th war. Among adult Jewish Israelis not directly exposed to the attacks, PTSD rates surged to 23%—five times higher than the pre-war rate of 4.5%. Clinical anxiety now affects 55% of adult Jewish Israelis, with 23% experiencing moderate to high levels. Young people and women exhibit the highest rates of PTSD.[3]

The National Center for Traumatic Stress and Resilience at Tel Aviv University projects at least 30,000 new PTSD cases—a conservative estimate. This surge comes when Israel's mental healthcare system is already stretched thin, with patients often waiting for several months for psychological care. While anxiety and depression respond well to treatment, with success rates around 70%, PTSD proves more resistant, with only 40% of patients showing improvement. Half of all referrals come from IDF reservists, with additional cases from Gaza area residents and Nova festival attack survivors.

The long-term implications are severe. Prof. Bar-Haim anticipates that this crisis will affect Israeli society for at least three decades, as some survivors develop symptoms years after their traumatic experiences.[4] Recent data from Statista reinforces this concern, showing Israel as the second most stressed nation globally, with 62% of its population reporting significant daily stress—surpassed only by Northern Cyprus at 65%.[5]

A Practical Approach to Healing

While meditation isn't a cure-all for these profound challenges, its advantages are evident: it boasts a substantial body of scientific research supporting its effectiveness, requires no expensive equipment, is easy to learn, and can be practiced independently. Studies indicate that regular practice can reduce anxiety symptoms by 30%–40%, and one preliminary analysis suggests that meditation may help manage PTSD symptoms.

In the following chapters, we explore the Rebbe's guidelines for kosher meditation, which provide a framework for safe and effective stress reduction. We examine stress's physiological effects before presenting specific techniques and their implementation. This isn't a book of theory—it's a practical manual for better living. You'll discover concrete meditation techniques, strategies for cognitive restructuring, and methods for building resilience. Each chapter builds on the previous one, creating a comprehensive approach to stress management and personal well-being.

Whether struggling with daily stress, dealing with anxiety, or simply seeking better ways to handle life's challenges, this book offers valuable tools and practical solutions. The methods described here honor Jewish law (Halakha) and are supported by scientific research. They provide a path toward enhanced physical and emotional well-being. The upcoming chapters will guide you in implementing these techniques step by step, teaching you a simple method of activating your natural relaxation response while preserving harmony with Jewish practice and tradition.

Chapter 1: The Lubavitcher Rebbe's Vision for Therapeutic Kosher Meditation

Historical Roots

As early as 1962, the Rebbe advocated for the development of therapeutic meditation to address what he termed "psychic stress." He asked Rabbi Dr. Abraham Twerski, a newly qualified psychiatrist, to develop a system of kosher meditation for this purpose. The Rebbe sent Dr. Twerski a paper on Eastern meditation, crossing out specific passages he deemed inappropriate and suggesting alternative phrasing in the margins.[1]

Dr. Twerski could not fulfill the Rebbe's request because establishing his medical practice demanded his attention, and he had no experience with meditation.

In March 1977, Israel's Sephardic Chief Rabbi Ovadiah Yosef issued a comprehensive *psak din* (religious ruling) that banned oriental (Eastern) meditation, gurus, and cults. He urged Jews everywhere to avoid association with these groups due to their idolatrous beliefs and practices.

However, the Rebbe's approach was more nuanced. In a letter to Rabbi Yaakov Landau, Chief Rabbi of B'nei Brak, the Rebbe acknowledged being aware of the *psak din*. Still, it clarified that the therapeutic benefits of meditation did not rely on the forbidden aspects. He suggested that it would be proper—and perhaps essential—for Rabbi Landau to use his influence to encourage G-d-fearing medical professionals who deal with the nervous system and emotional well-being to study and publish findings on how seclusion and self-contemplation could treat ailments that impact the nervous system, emotional well-being, and mental health.

In addition to healing many who need such therapies, the Rebbe wrote that the options would disconnect some Jews from the gurus who lured them with promises of better health and success in school or business.[2]

Recognizing the therapeutic benefits of meditation in addressing the widespread stress of the mid-1970s, the Rebbe, while acknowledging the prohibition of Eastern meditation practices under Jewish law, sought to create a kosher form of meditation free from idolatrous associations, providing a safe alternative for Jews drawn to the Eastern cults, prevalent at the time, that promised stress relief.

In a public talk about kosher meditation delivered on 13 Tammuz, 5739 (July 8, 1979) (see Appendix A), the Rebbe stated,

> Every facet of life can be used in a positive way or in an opposite direction. For example, the sun, the moon, and the stars are necessary for life of earth. They bring about manifold goodness. However, they also have been worshipped as false gods. One might

ask (as the Talmud asks): "Since they have been worshipped as false gods, shouldn't they be destroyed? However, should G-d destroy the world because of the foolishness of the idol-worshipers?" The same concept applies in regard to meditation. Though essentially good, meditation can also be destructive.

The Cover Letter and the Memorandum

In January 1978, the Lubavitcher Rebbe wrote a confidential memorandum concerning the growing influence of Eastern spiritual practices on Jewish communities. This document and a cover letter were sent to approximately fifty mental health specialists, including psychiatrists, neurologists, and psychologists.

The Cover Letter

The cover letter, dated Teveth 5738 (December 1978), explained the Rebbe's decision to leave the memorandum unsigned and separate from the cover letter.

The Rebbe expressed two primary concerns.

First, by acknowledging that certain meditation practices could offer therapeutic benefits for stress relief, there was a risk of inadvertently legitimizing these movements, which could lead people to cultic involvement.

Second, since kosher therapeutic meditation alternatives were not readily available at that time, individuals might be tempted to engage with non-Jewish meditation practices, believing they could separate the therapeutic elements from the idolatrous components—a distinction the Rebbe considered practically impossible to maintain.

The cover letter characterized the situation as spiritual *Pikuach-Nefesh* (preservation of life). He expressed his commitment to mobilizing all possible resources, even at the risk of duplicating efforts. (See Appendix A, Letter 2 for the complete document.)

The Memorandum

The memorandum conveyed the Rebbe's deep concern that in the mid-1970s, tens of thousands of Jews were engaging in Eastern spiritual practices, particularly Transcendental Meditation and yoga. Rabbinic authorities categorized these practices as Avodah Zarah (idolatry). The religious nature of Transcendental Meditation was legally recognized by the United States Federal Court in Malnak v. Maharishi Mahesh Yogi (U.S.D.C. of N.J. 76-341). The Rebbe attached the Court's decision to the memorandum.

Recognizing the therapeutic benefits of meditation for stress relief, the memorandum urged medical professionals to develop secular meditation alternatives that would harness these benefits while eliminating the problematic aspects. The document outlined three specific recommendations:

- Medical professionals should research and develop stress-relief techniques based on meditation practices.

- Doctors should incorporate these "kosher" methods in their standard medical practice.
- Doctors should actively promote and publicize these kosher alternatives to the popular Eastern meditations that were prevalent at the time.

Urgency

The Rebbe maintained that sufficient research already existed to support the effectiveness of meditation in reducing stress. He recognized that traditional academic channels would proceed too slowly to address the urgent situation at hand. Rather than waiting for additional peer-reviewed studies, he advocated for prompt action based on the existing evidence of meditation's stress-relief benefits. The Rebbe's message was clear: when confronting a threat to Jewish spiritual welfare, taking actions that might help—even without guaranteed success—was not only permissible but essential.

As stated in the memorandum (see Appendix A, Letter 1 for the complete document):

> Needless to say, even if one feels doubtful whether he can advance this cause, or whether the expectation warrants the effort—the vital importance and urgency of saving so many souls from Avodah Zarah, not only warrants but dictates every possible effort, even if there be a doubt about achieving success; certainly when there is every reason to believe that much, indeed, can be achieved,

with G-d's help and Zechus Harabbim (the merit of the many).

Dr. Yehuda Landes, a clinical psychologist in Palo Alto, California, was one of the few who responded to the memorandum, initiating a lengthy correspondence with the Rebbe. Their discussions primarily focused on establishing a Jewish Meditation Institute offering an alternative to Transcendental Meditation. On two occasions, the Rebbe offered start-up funding for the Institute.

An ad hoc committee, which included Dr. Landes, Dr. Chaim (Charles) Rosen, and Dr. Seymour Applebaum, was formed to explore this possibility. As detailed in *"The Inside Story of the Founding of Jewish Meditation"* by Rabbi Yehoshua Landes, Dr. Landes's son, the Rebbe ultimately determined that establishing the Institute would be impractical.[3] The projected costs were too high, the timeline too long, and the potential reach too limited to have a meaningful impact.

In response to these challenges, the Rebbe adjusted his strategy by encouraging professionals who already offered clinically effective meditation techniques to publicize them and encourage others to do the same. Drs. Landes and Rosen tried to advance the initiative with meditation workshops in California and New York, but these efforts were short-lived due to a lack of interest and support.

Understanding Kosher Meditation's Distinct Purpose

Kosher meditation differs from contemplative Jewish practices like hisbonenus, which is structured and intellectual (focused on understanding), and hitbodedut—spontaneous, open, and direct communication with G-d involving solitude and personal expression. It also differs from meditations rooted in mystical texts such as the Kabbalah and Zohar.

While these practices have been foundational to Judaism for thousands of years, the meditation described here has one primary purpose: to trigger the relaxation response, the body's natural counterbalance to stress. To illustrate the healing potential of effective kosher meditation, consider that, according to Stanford Medicine, most medical textbooks link 50%–80% of all diseases to stress-related origins.[4]

Implementation and Benefits

It is recommended that you meditate for 15 to 20 minutes twice a day. This is a significant amount of time, especially for busy and stressed individuals, so the investment needs to be worthwhile. Chapter 12 reviews extensive research conducted at some of the world's leading universities on the well-documented benefits of meditation on health. Hopefully, it will persuade you to give it a try.

You will also learn how to incorporate meditation into your daily routine, creating moments of calm amidst life's chaos.

Whether dealing with work-related stress, family or financial pressures, or seeking inner peace, this book offers a way forward.

Beyond Meditation: A Complete Healing Framework

However, this book is not only about meditation. We have incorporated two additional powerful tools from the Rebbe's healing approach: nurturing positive thinking and learning to trust our innate healing abilities. These concepts extend beyond mere feel-good sentiments—when paired with regular meditation, they create a synergistic framework for improved health and well-being.

Think of this book as a user manual for activating your mind's natural stress-relief system. There's no mysticism or complicated philosophy—just effective techniques that align with Jewish law and deliver real results.

For those considering meditation for health reasons, it is strongly recommended to consult with your healthcare provider (see Appendix B). While I have made every effort to ensure that all recommendations are free from elements of Avodah Zarah (idolatry), please seek guidance from a religious authority with expertise in this area if you have specific concerns.

Chapter 2:
The Impact of Stress on Health and Well-Being

Before learning about meditation, this chapter provides detailed scientific information on how stress affects the body. You don't have to read it thoroughly if you're not interested; the main points will be clear even if you skim the technical details. You don't need to understand how the engine works to be a good driver.

Stress and Your Body

Stress is the natural reaction your body experiences when changes or challenges arise. It can lead to various physical, emotional, and behavioral responses. [1] It is an unavoidable part of human existence. While we typically manage everyday pressures, significant life events—such as career changes, job loss, marriage, divorce, illness, financial troubles, losing a loved one, or natural disasters—can trigger intense stress responses. The constant 24/7 news cycle and the overwhelming influx of information in our digital age only amplify these stressors.

Biological Stress Response

The body's stress response mechanism, known as the "fight-or-flight" response, was first identified over 100 years ago by Harvard professor Walter Cannon. It encompasses a complex system of physiological adaptations that trigger a cascade of hormonal reactions, primarily releasing adrenaline (epinephrine) and noradrenaline (norepinephrine) into the bloodstream. These hormones initiate physiological changes, including increased heart rate, accelerated breathing, higher blood pressure, and improved blood flow to the muscles—all of which prepare the body to respond to the threat at hand. [2.]

Neural Mechanisms

The sympathetic nervous system, a component of the autonomic nervous system, orchestrates these involuntary responses through specific brain regions. The thalamus processes sensory information and relays it to the amygdala—the brain's fear center—while the hypothalamus maintains homeostasis by regulating autonomic functions and hormone production.[3] This sophisticated neural network enables rapid threat assessment and response, a crucial evolutionary adaptation for survival.[4]

Health Implications of Chronic Stress

Individual stress susceptibility varies based on psychological and physiological factors, but research demonstrates that prolonged stress can ultimately overwhelm anyone.[5] The effects are observed in multiple systems.

Physical Impact

- **Musculoskeletal System:** Ongoing muscle tension leading to headache, back pain, and temporomandibular joint disorders (a collection of conditions that impact the joints and muscles of the jaw)
- **Cardiovascular System:** Increased risk of blood clots from heightened platelet adhesion during adrenaline surges; raised blood pressure affecting vital organs
- **Immune System:** Although chronic inflammation is beneficial in acute situations for combating pathogens, it can become persistent and lead to atherosclerosis (a chronic disease that occurs when plaque builds up in the walls of the arteries, making them narrow and stiff) and various other diseases.

Hormonal and Neurological Effects

- **Cortisol Release:** This primary stress hormone can trigger several adverse effects, including:
    - Muscle and bone weakness
    - Compromised immune function
    - Cognitive impairment, particularly memory
    - Disrupted sleep patterns
    - Increased appetite
- **Brain Function:** Stress can impair the prefrontal cortex, impacting essential cognitive functions such as decision making, judgment, and ethical reasoning.

Behavioral Impact

Stress often leads to detrimental lifestyle changes, including:

- Poor dietary choices, particularly increased consumption of processed foods
- Reduced physical activity
- Inadequate sleep
- Increased substance use
- Psychological manifestations such as anxiety and depression

While many stressors—whether global events, such as pandemics and natural disasters, or personal challenges—are beyond individual control, understanding their physiological impact is essential for developing effective coping strategies and maintaining overall well-being.

Chapter 3:
The Relaxation Response: Harnessing the Power of the Mind

Dr. Herbert Benson (1935–2022), a Harvard cardiologist and pioneer of mind-body medicine, made a groundbreaking discovery in the 1970s—a natural antidote to the fight-or-flight response. He identified a natural state he initially termed a "wakeful hypometabolic state," later simplified to "the relaxation response"—an automatic response that triggers the body's self-healing mechanism to combat stress.[1]

The significance of his work became evident through subsequent research. A landmark study in 1981 revealed that 60% to 90% of doctor visits were related to stress and somatization, which involves recurrent and multiple medical symptoms with no identifiable, organic cause. A similar investigation in 1989 showed that only 16% of common complaints during physician visits had identifiable physical causes over a three-year period, with the remainder likely linked to stress and psychosocial factors.[2]

A New Paradigm in Health and Wellness

For over 50 years, Dr. Benson and his colleagues at Harvard and Massachusetts General Hospital researched the effect of eliciting the relaxation response on numerous illnesses and disease processes caused or complicated by stress. Their findings appeared in some of the world's top medical journals. Harvard Medical School also now advocates the same cross-disciplinary linkages Benson encouraged throughout his career.

An Antidote to the Fight-or-Flight Response

Most of us experience the fight-or-flight mobilization several times a day when challenged by stressful situations. Sometimes felt as a burst of adrenaline, the reaction includes increased blood pressure, blood flow to the muscles, breath rate, heart rate, and metabolism. As mentioned earlier, the fight-or-flight response is an innate defense mechanism that prepares the body to stand its ground and fight or flee to a place of safety.[3] Unfortunately, in our fast-paced, anxiety-filled lives, the stress response gets triggered too often, and our nervous system gets overloaded. Paradoxically, this safety mechanism that is critical for survival is also responsible for many illnesses through its too-frequent daily activation.

Discovering the Relaxation Response

Some 50 years after Cannon, Dr. Benson, then a young research cardiologist in the same Harvard laboratory, discovered a method to trigger a completely opposite physiological response. He initially employed Transcendental Meditation (TM), a Hindu-based practice that incorporates a mantra (a Sanskrit word or sound repeated during meditation) to activate this response.[4] Benson had been invited to examine the physiological changes in a group of experienced TM practitioners who volunteered to participate. Within minutes of starting their meditation, physiological and metabolic measures indicated that the volunteers were resting at a level that surpassed even the deepest stage of natural sleep.

Benson realized he was measuring a unique phenomenon markedly different from the universally familiar three states of consciousness: awake, sleeping, and dreaming. Benson believed he had identified an integrated response opposite the fight-or-flight response.[5] He described the physiological changes of the relaxation response as being associated with what has been called an altered state of consciousness. In Benson's description, it is an *altered* state simply because it is not our everyday experience and must be consciously and purposefully evoked.[6]

Creating a Universal Protocol for Triggering the Relaxation Response

As a cardiologist and researcher, Benson understood the relaxation response's potential to improve the lives of millions of people suffering from stress-related illnesses. He needed a simple, reliable means to activate the response that would be more practical and broadly appealing than spiritual practices like TM. *The Relaxation Response*, Benson's first book, recounts how he and his colleagues developed that protocol.

Benson dedicated over a year to studying Eastern and Western religions. Despite their diverse faiths and cultures, they all included some form of meditation. Many used prayer, rituals, medicinal plants, and other methods to escape daily activities by triggering a relaxation response. Whether for spiritual enlightenment or mental well-being, individuals from diverse backgrounds have historically found ways to retreat from life's demands, entering a state of tranquility. By recognizing the universality of the ability to move into this peaceful detachment, Benson suggested that the relaxation response could be an effective antidote to stress.[7]

Taking the Research to the Heights

A few years later, Benson studied advanced forms of meditation practiced by Tibetan monks living in exile in India. The first researchers to measure the monks' physiology while meditating, he and his team carried scientific equipment and supplies to altitudes of 15,000 feet in the Himalayas.[8]

In a striking demonstration of the power of the mind, the monks, wearing small loincloths in freezing temperatures, first draped themselves in soaking wet sheets and then used a heat-producing meditation to raise their body temperature. Within a few minutes, they emitted enough heat to produce steam and dry the sheets.

When interviewed, the monks said they first used a relaxation response technique to quiet their minds. Next, they visualized fire or heat traveling through a central channel in their bodies. This description inspired Benson to explore visualization as a second stage in his relaxation response protocol, which he more fully described in his book *Relaxation Revolution: The Science and Genetics of Mind Body Healing*.[9]

Three Milestones That Put It All Together

Milestone 1: Discovering the Relaxation Response

In *The Relaxation Revolution*, Dr. Benson describes the relaxation response as the opposite of the fight-or-flight or stress response and characterizes the state as follows:

- Decreased metabolism, heart rate, blood pressure, and rate of breathing
- A decrease or calming in brain activity
- An increase in the attention and decision-making functions of the brain
- Changes in gene activity that are opposite to those associated with stress [10]

Benson wanted to identify what triggered the relaxation response and whether the observed physiological changes in TM could be replicated in an easy-to-learn manner that produced consistent results. TM couldn't be used because its focus words (mantras) were proprietary. In addition, TM's initiation ceremony was problematic. The ceremony consists of devotional acts chanted in Sanskrit by the TM instructor, while repeated offerings are placed on an altar to deities before an image of a dead guru. This ritual is a sanctified, inviolable part of TM instruction (see chapter 15).

Benson's subsequent research demonstrated that the identical physiological results observed in the TM subjects could be consistently triggered without TM mantras or Hindu ceremonies; all that mattered was thinking a focus word and returning to it upon noticing when the mind had drifted to a thought. He initially used the word "one" to replace the TM mantra and published his findings in a 1974 issue of *Psychiatry*.[11] Later, Benson found that the relaxation response could be triggered simply by repeating any focus word or even engaging in a repetitive physical activity like walking, swimming, jogging, knitting, or rowing. The triggering process remained the same: returning to the focus word or activity when one's awareness had become engaged in a thought or the activity.[12]

Benson did not claim to have discovered something new. Eliciting the relaxation response has occurred over the ages but has merely faded from modern life. However, he believed it would re-emerge once people understood that gaining the benefits of meditation does not require religious rituals, beliefs, or esoteric practices.

Benson's groundbreaking book, *The Relaxation Response* (1975), was an unexpected runaway *New York Times* bestseller. By the year 2000, it had been reprinted 38 times, selling nearly four million copies, with translations in 13 languages. For two years, it was the self-care book most often recommended by health professionals.[13]

Milestone 2: The Healing Power of Expectation and Belief

Benson's second significant contribution was to renew an appreciation for the power of faith and belief in healing. In his book *Timeless Healing, the Power of Biology and Belief* (1996), he explores the healing power of faith and belief, concluding that when in crisis, people often turn to religion and faith, which frequently play an essential role in restoring health.[14] Benson also describes the synergistic value of faith and belief when combined with relaxation training. Together, they often produce better outcomes than either factor alone (see more on this topic in Chapter 9).

Milestone 3: Switching Genes On and Off

In the *Relaxation Revolution: The Science and Genetics of Mind Body Healing* (2010), Benson presents groundbreaking research on the relaxation response's ability to "switch on" beneficial gene expression and "switch off" harmful gene expression. You may not be able to change your genes, but you can use your mind to change how the genes you do have are switched on and off, which can enhance your potential for health and healing.[15]

Physiological Impact: Changes in Metabolism and Neurology

Sleep vs. Meditation

Some of Benson's early research focused on the factors differentiating the relaxation response from sleep. Sleep enables the body to recover from daily activities by promoting muscle relaxation, cell repair, and memory consolidation.

Experiments comparing sleep and meditation demonstrated a significant reduction in the body's oxygen consumption during meditation. This condition of notably lowered metabolism, known as "hypometabolism," is exceptionally restful.

To draw a comparison, oxygen consumption typically decreases by about 8% from wakeful levels after four to five hours of sleep. However, skilled meditators experience reductions in oxygen consumption within the first several minutes, averaging a decrease of 10% to 20%. This remarkable change requires activating a relaxation response. For instance, when you hold your breath, your tissues maintain the same rate of oxygen consumption until the oxygen is completely depleted. Nevertheless, the rate of oxygen consumption does not decrease.[16]

Brain Activity

Changes in brain activity patterns also occur during meditation. Electroencephalogram (EEG) studies have found fundamental differences between the brain wave patterns in meditation and sleep. Alpha waves (8–12 Hz) increase in intensity and frequency during meditation but do not commonly appear in sleep. The significance of alpha waves is still being researched, but they are associated with feeling calmer and less anxious.

Other patterns also differ between those observed during meditation and those found during sleep. For instance, rapid eye movement (REM)—characteristic of sleep and often linked to dreaming—is nonexistent or happens significantly less in meditation.[17]

Reduced Blood Lactate Levels

Studies have also shown that blood lactate levels, which can be associated with anxiety and are also known to rise during vigorous exercise, decrease significantly within the first 10 minutes of meditating. The reduction is consistent with reduced activity in the sympathetic nervous system.[18]

Molecular Changes

Benson's team observed molecular changes, including increased exhaled nitric oxide (NO), supporting the hypothesis that the NO molecule may positively impact the body's antibacterial, antiviral, and stress responses. The release of NO, facilitated by the relaxation response, could help protect the body from microbial infections, cardiovascular problems (e.g., hypertension), and immune system problems.[19] Subsequent research continues to bolster this hypothesis.[20]

Effects on Brain Function and Structure

Another research team used functional magnetic resonance imaging (fMRI) to explore whether meditation might be associated with physical changes in the brain. The procedure involved 20 individuals with extensive meditation experience and 15 matched controls with no meditation background. fMRI detected changes related to blood flow to create a picture of brain activity.

Three-dimensional imaging of participants' brains found that those who regularly elicited the relaxation response through different techniques had thicker cortices (the decision-making region of the brain) in areas associated with attention, sensory, cognitive, and emotional processing. Greater cortical thickness in the older participants' brains suggested that meditation might offset age-related cortical thinning.[21]

More Work on Gene Expression

Benson's exploration of mind–body healing reached a pivotal moment in 2008 when he and seven co-authors published "Genomic Counter-Stress Changes Induced by the Relaxation Response." This study delivered a powerful conclusion: mind–body practices can "turn on" and "turn off" disease-associated genes, effectively altering how those genes are activated or expressed. The findings validated Benson's commitment to understanding the connection between mental and physical well-being.[22]

Researchers investigated the blood samples from three groups: long-term practitioners of relaxation techniques, a control group with no prior experience, and a second control group that underwent eight weeks of relaxation training. They discovered significant differences in the gene expression profiles between the long-term practitioners and those with no experience. Surprisingly, after just eight weeks of training, the second control group displayed similar changes in gene expression, though not as pronounced as those seen in the long-term practitioners.

The affected genes were primarily those involved in cellular metabolism and the body's response to oxidative stress, which can be damaged by long-term exposure to stress. The researchers hypothesized that practicing relaxation techniques may enhance the body's ability to deal with stress on a molecular level, potentially countering stress-related harm.

Both novice and experienced practitioners experienced significant changes in gene expression, showing improvements in critical areas for cellular health and function, like metabolism and oxidative stress management. The study provides initial evidence that regularly participating in practices that induce the relaxation response can alter gene expression, possibly safeguarding against the harmful effects of stress.

The implications of this research are enormous: the mind, through various relaxation techniques, can influence the body down to the genetic level. The study paves the way for a more integrative approach to health that embraces the importance of relaxation practices in fostering healing and resilience.

The pioneering work of Dr. Herbert Benson and his colleagues has significantly advanced our understanding of the mind-body connection. By providing a scientific foundation for employing simple methods to combat stress and promote well-being without relying on specific cultural or religious practices, Benson made the advantages of deep relaxation accessible to a wide audience. Furthermore, his insights into the power of belief and expectation in healing have underscored the importance of integrating psychological and emotional factors into health management.

Finally, Benson's research on gene expression has opened the door to the potential of the mind–body approach to enhance the effectiveness of conventional medicine in powerful ways that we are only beginning to understand.

Benson's work continues to inspire further exploration into how we can harness our innate capacity for self-healing. Indeed, the mind's power over the body is profound, and cultivating optimal health and longevity is within our reach. These discoveries underscore the powerful connection between our mental state and physical well-being, suggesting that the path to healing may be found in the stillness of our minds.

Chapter 4: The Rebbe's Meditation Guidelines

Before diving into the meditation technique outlined in Chapter 5, let's address two essential basics: who this practice is suitable for, according to the Rebbe's guidelines, and how to prepare yourself for success. Consider this your pre-flight checklist—the key information you need before getting started.

Understanding the Rebbe's Vision

The Rebbe approached meditation from a unique perspective, viewing it not as a threat to Judaism but as a therapeutic tool with proven stress-relief benefits.

Two primary objectives guided the Rebbe's meditation framework:

1. Provide therapeutic stress relief for individuals experiencing anxiety from business worries, family issues, health concerns, and other stressors that reduce their quality of life.

2. Develop kosher alternatives to the widespread idolatrous meditation practices of the 1970s that were attracting tens of thousands of Jewish youth and adults.

The Therapeutic Framework

The Rebbe emphasized that kosher meditation is therapeutic rather than spiritual. The goal is to achieve psychological health and peace of mind for those who lack it.

> There are certain aspects of psychological health and tranquility that can be attained by taking oneself out of contact with the surrounding hullabaloo and tumult of life. By retreating into solitude (not necessarily leaving the city) and by withdrawing into seclusion for a period of time, one may attain psychological health and peace of mind. This manner of behavior strengthens the individual and guards his mental health. This process involves withdrawing from the clamor and tumult of the street and meditating on an object that brings about serenity and peace of mind.[1]

He specifically cautioned against conflating kosher meditation with meditations found in Jewish mystical traditions.

> The intent is not that you should teach Kabbalah or Chassidus or Torah in general, but only and exclusively teach meditation and mental concentration and the like such as are kosher and permissible according to the Shulchan Aruch—it is possible to attain peace of mind, etc. Especially to attain peace

of mind by those in whom this is acutely lacking, due to anxiety in business, Sholom Bayis, health, and similar stresses.[2]

The Rebbe's stance on meditation reflected careful deliberation. While never explicitly endorsing specific techniques, his correspondence revealed a sophisticated approach to what he termed "Kosher meditation," a practice that preserved meditation's therapeutic benefits while eliminating idolatrous elements.

His approach was nuanced. While he accepted certain Jewish elements if they enhanced appeal, he intentionally avoided incorporating overtly Jewish themes or rituals. This addressed a practical concern: too much religious content could deter the very Jews he wanted to dissuade from Eastern cults, as they might view the practice as merely a pathway to increased religious observance. His caution against using the term "mysticism" indicated a wariness of unwanted associations with both Jewish and non-Jewish mystical traditions.

In December 1978, Dr. Landes presented the Rebbe with a pilot meditation program aimed at distinguishing it from Eastern practices. Instead of emptying the mind—which he considered central to Eastern meditation—the program encouraged focusing on specific concepts, such as Hebrew letters, the S'hma, or visual elements like Shabbat candles. He also created a breathing exercise using Ha'Shem ("Ha" for inhaling, "Shem" for exhaling).

TM as Shorthand for "Values Free"

In a letter to Dr. Landes dated 19 Shevat 5739 (February 16, 1979), the Rebbe responded through his secretary,

> In regards to your activities: Continue (in T.M.) and the need for this only grew. [In turn], the merit and power given from above to you, and those helping you, likewise grew. (In regards to what you wrote that you are doing this in a 'Kosher way' [the Rebbe noted]): And continue to do so, for this is necessary for those individuals—in order for them to be suitable and prepared for *Dveykus* (communion with G-d) etc.

The statement "continue in TM" may initially appear to endorse TM. However, this was not the Rebbe's intention. Dr. Landes had explicitly labeled TM as the most prominent and dangerous among meditation cults— a view shared by the Rebbe, who described TM as a new plague affecting Jewish youth.

The Rebbe seemingly used "TM" as shorthand for the values-free meditation he envisioned. His endorsement of a TM-type approach, along with his silence about the breathing exercise, suggests that his primary interest was in developing meditation techniques stripped of idolatrous elements that could effectively address stress and provide an alternative for Jews seeking relief from non-kosher sources.

The confidential memorandum (see Appendix A, Letter 1) provides another example of TM as shorthand. The Rebbe acknowledged that some physicians discreetly used TM-like methods, typically as adjuncts to conventional treatment.

Herbert Benson's 1975 bestseller, The Relaxation Response, offered a well-researched, clinically validated, and compelling secular adaptation of TM. While undoubtedly aware of Benson's method, the Rebbe continued to explore alternatives, leading him to write the confidential memorandum that resulted in his extensive correspondence with Dr. Landes in the late 1970s.

The Rebbe was addressing two distinct yet interconnected issues. While Benson's value-free approach might assist individuals in managing daily stress, it couldn't compete with TM's mystical cultural appeal for young Jews exploring meditation. The competition was intense, and the problem had reached epidemic proportions. In 1968, the Beatles' visit to the TM ashram in India ignited a surge in TM's popularity in Western countries. In 1977, celebrity endorsements and media attention resulted in over 300,000 Americans learning Transcendental Meditation (TM)—among them, tens of thousands of Jews.

I believe this recognition fueled the Rebbe's desire to create kosher meditation practices that mirrored popular Eastern methods while carefully avoiding their problematic aspects.

The Rebbe's search continued. In 1981, he asked Mrs. Atara Hasofer to find a neutral meditation. Her daughter, Chabad

Shlucha Chaya Kaye from Sydney, Australia, shared the following story with me.

> My father was a professor of statistics, highly sought after by many international universities, and was invited by many to spend a sabbatical year. So, when my parents were in the yechidus (private meeting with Rebbe), my father mentioned two options for a nine-month Sabbatical: one was in Malaysia, and I don't know what the other one was. The Rebbe told them they should take the one at the University of Penang in Malaysia and that while my father was there, my mother should investigate finding a neutral meditation.

The Rebbe may have concluded that a meditation promoted by a Harvard research professor couldn't compete with TM's appeal. This may explain why he emphasized that kosher meditation should resemble popular Eastern meditation methods as much as possible while carefully avoiding their problematic elements.

A Kosher Approach: Stress Relief Through a Simple Meditation Technique

I believe the meditation described in this book aligns with the Rebbe's guidelines. It is similar to the technique I learned when I became a TM teacher and to Benson's method of eliciting the relaxation response, which was also based on the TM method.

While researching this book, I discovered that the technique is not exclusive to TM; many meditation practices taught in India are similar or identical to it. However, all objectionable elements have been removed, leaving only the core technique essential for relieving stress by eliciting the relaxation response.

- There are no initiation ceremonies, Hindu mantras, cult exposure, or any Eastern influences.
- You select your own focus word. Suggestions for focus words in Chapter 5 include either Hebrew words or neutral English words, or you can create your own.
- The meditation is self-directed. You learn how to meditate by following the detailed instructions in this book or watching the animation.
- A vast amount of research shows that the recommended meditation method effectively reduces stress.

The Rebbe's Meditation Guidelines

The Medical Perspective

The Rebbe viewed meditation through a medical lens, likening it to prescription medication that requires careful consideration of dosage and timing. Just as a doctor prescribes medicine, the Rebbe advocated for meditation only as long as it remained beneficial as a therapeutic tool rather than a long-term lifestyle practice.

Who Should Consider Meditation?

The Rebbe's guidance was clear and practical. He recognized the benefits of meditation for those who faced:

- Anxiety and stress connected to business or financial matters
- Family tensions
- Health challenges
- Challenges in earning a living
- Mental or emotional distress
- Difficulty maintaining focus in spiritual service

The Rebbe advised against regular meditation for those already leading productive lives—individuals who successfully manage their work, family, and community responsibilities. However, he permitted meditation for anyone who felt compelled to pursue it and believed it would enhance their lives.

The Prescription Approach

Like any medication, the Rebbe stressed the importance of the proper "dosage." The Rebbe likely envisioned a future where healthcare providers would understand the health benefits of meditation and could tailor their patients' meditation practices accordingly. Unfortunately, this has not come to pass, leaving them unable to guide their patients appropriately. Even more troubling, some providers who are aware of meditation's benefits might unintentionally recommend practices associated with Avodah Zarah.

We recommend meditating for 15 to 20 minutes in each session, which is generally safe for most individuals. If you experience significant discomfort that continues despite attempting shorter meditation periods, please stop meditating.

- **Frequency:** Two times a day
- **Duration of Practice:** Temporary, not permanent—continue until the presenting issue resolves
- **Flexibility:** Resume if symptoms reappear

In Summary

The Rebbe wanted healthcare providers to be knowledgeable about kosher meditation and incorporate it into their practices. While this integration has not yet happened, his framework remains a balanced approach that:

- recognizes the therapeutic benefits of meditation,
- establishes clear guidelines for its use,
- emphasizes the temporary nature of the practice, and
- focuses on specific healing objectives.

Kosher meditation omits several elements found in other meditation traditions. These omissions ensure alignment with Jewish religious principles:

1. No initiation rituals or ceremonies

2. No traditional meditation accessories, such as bells or chimes
3. No religious gestures or expressions from non-Jewish traditions
4. No burning of incense
5. No bowing or kneeling
6. No representations of deities or religious imagery, regardless of their size or placement

The Rebbe's approach is that meditation, although powerful, should be a tool for healing, not a permanent fixture in our daily lives. It's about achieving the right balance—using meditation when necessary to remain actively engaged in our responsibilities.

For those contemplating meditation, the key is to evaluate your needs honestly: Do you need this tool for healing, or are you already doing well? Your response to this question should inform your decision to incorporate meditation into your life.

Chapter 5:
Preparing to Meditate

The Essence of Meditation

Meditation uses a focus word or a repetitive activity to help the mind disengage from the constant flow of thoughts that typically occupy it. As this happens, the mind naturally calms down, and the body relaxes due to the connection between the mind and body.

Here's how to meditate - it's simpler than you might think:

Pick a word or short phrase that feels calming to you. This will be your anchor - you'll return to it again and again.

Get comfortable and close your eyes. Think of your chosen word—not out loud, just in your head.

Your mind will wander. That's totally normal – it happens to everyone. You might start thinking about dinner, that email you need to send, or that embarrassing thing you did in third grade.

When you notice you're lost in thought, just guide your attention back to your word. Don't get frustrated - think of it like this: if you're paddling a canoe and drift off course, you'd make a slight adjustment to get back on track.

Keep at it - notice when your mind wanders, then return to your word. That's all meditation really is. Do this for however long you planned to meditate.

Meditation isn't about doing it perfectly or stilling the mind; it's about effortlessly returning to your chosen focus whenever you notice your attention has drifted from it. Though meditation techniques vary widely, many share this fundamental mechanism of gentle refocusing.

Choosing Your Focus Word

Your focus word—a word or short phrase you repeat mentally—is the heart of your meditation practice. It allows your mind to settle inward to a calmer place. Any word or short phrase that feels calming will work.

The word's sound value matters more than its meaning. Some people prefer a focus word with religious or spiritual connotations, while others prefer a secular word. It is your choice; either option is fine.

A few suggestions are provided below, but feel free to select any word you prefer. Any word or phrase you choose should avoid harsh or complex pronunciations or negative associations.

Hebrew Suggestions

Echod (one), *Shalom* (peace), *S'hma* (Hear), *or S'hma Yisroel* (Hear O Israel), *bitachon* (trust), and *emunah* (faith)

English Suggestions

Love, Peace, Gentle, Kind, Kindness, Relax, Calm, Be calm, or Ease

Review the suggestions above and softly repeat the words aloud or in your mind. When you find one that resonates with you, choose that word as your focus. You may want to jot it down to help you remember it.

Kosher meditation is a therapeutic method for reducing stress, unlike Jewish contemplative or mystical meditations, which are aimed at spiritual objectives. Although this meditation is not designed to enhance religious experiences, any practice that fosters inner peace and heightens awareness will naturally enrich one's religious life. Therefore, while more meaningful religious practices and spiritual experiences are not the main goals, they may be welcome byproducts.

Understanding the Role of Thoughts

The connection between thoughts and meditation is often misunderstood. Rather than seeing thoughts as interruptions, acknowledge them as essential to your meditation. Picture your mind as a city street—some days, mental traffic flows easily, while on other days, you might feel stuck in traffic. Both experiences are equally valid.

The essence of meditation is not maintaining uninterrupted focus but gently returning to your focus word when you notice your mind has wandered from it. This natural alternation between your focus word and other thoughts allows the mind to settle down and elicits the relaxation response.

Setting Realistic Expectations

A common pitfall for new meditators is striving for the "perfect" meditation. This mindset often results in unnecessary self-judgment and counterproductive attempts to force the process. It's important to understand that relaxation is a natural outcome of meditation, not a precursor.

Creating the Best Conditions for Success

Meditation is most effective when you create an environment that supports it. Here are several suggestions that many people have found beneficial. Some may work for you, while others may not.

Taking Sensible Precautions

Due to its relaxing effects, avoid meditation while operating vehicles or machinery. For optimal results, steer clear of recreational drugs for several weeks before beginning your practice. It's best to avoid meditating while under the influence of alcohol.

When Is the Best Time to Meditate?

Most people find that meditating first thing in the morning before breakfast works best. To fully wake up from sleep, you may want to splash a little water on your face, stretch a bit, etc. Then, sit up in bed or on your chair, close your eyes, take a few breaths, and begin.

What if morning meditation doesn't work for you? Everyone's schedule and biorhythms are different. If morning meditation isn't your thing, consider alternatives, like meditating after breakfast. Have a light breakfast without caffeine and wait 15–30 minutes after eating to minimize digestive distractions. A mid-morning meditation can work if you have time after finishing your morning routine.

It's important to remember that meditation is a personal practice. There isn't a one-size-fits-all answer for the best time to meditate. Experiment with different times to find what works best for your lifestyle and energy level. Listen to your body, consider your schedule, and be patient with yourself. Pay attention to how food or caffeine in your stomach affects your meditation, as this can guide you on how long to wait before meditating after a meal. The goal is to make meditation a comfortable habit you look forward to rather than a chore.

Your Second Meditation of the Day (or the Next Morning)

Allow eight hours between your morning and evening meditations, give or take. If you meditate in the morning, it's best to have your second meditation before dinner. However, if that timing isn't feasible and you have a full meal, wait about an hour after eating for digestion to settle before meditating. If your first meditation was in the evening, the second should be in the morning.

Creating an Environment for Success

Minimizing Distractions

Create a meditation-friendly space; choose a quiet area with a comfortable temperature and subdued lighting. Ask your family or roommates not to disturb you for 15 to 20 minutes. Close the door to keep pets away. Turn off your cell phone and other electronic devices.

No matter how carefully you prepare, you can count on being interrupted. Most interruptions are minor and can be ignored or managed without disrupting your meditation. If an interruption becomes too disruptive, pause your meditation momentarily until you feel centered, then continue. If you need to leave your meditation, return when possible to complete your session.

When we had young children, my wife and I sometimes took turns meditating in the car, which was quiet and free from interruptions. If you work in an office with a private space, consider arriving early and staying late so you can meditate there.

As your practice deepens, external sounds and conversations become less disruptive. Treat environmental disturbances like your thoughts—acknowledge their presence without actively engaging or resisting them. The key is to gently return to your focus word whenever you notice that your attention has drifted, no matter the cause, including noise.

Chapter 6:
Your First Meditation

As you begin your first meditation, you should be in a quiet room, having taken reasonable steps to minimize interruptions. Loosen any tight clothing. If you're sitting in a chair, both feet should rest on the floor. If you're seated on a bed, sofa, or a roomy chair, you can sit cross-legged or in any comfortable position.

You will have chosen a focus word to repeat mentally while you meditate (see Chapter 5).

Set a gentle timer—your phone on vibrate or a quiet alarm works well—for 10 minutes. This frees your mind from worrying about time. If you live with others, they can quietly let you when the time is up.

If you prefer, you can place a clock where you can see it and peek occasionally with one eye. Skip any harsh alarms that might jolt you out of your calm state. Don't worry too much about timing, though—after a few weeks of regular practice, you'll naturally sense when your session is over.

When the time is up, keep your eyes closed while you gradually let go of the focus word and begin to favor regular thoughts. Take a minute or two to slowly return to the everyday world. Then, gently open your eyes, bit by bit, as if you're watching the dawn breaking.

Your First 10-Minute Meditation

Find a comfortable, seated position and close your eyes. Let your body relax naturally. As thoughts drift through your mind, simply let them pass by like clouds in the sky. After settling in for a minute or so, begin to mentally repeat your focus word, without moving your tongue or lips—just let the word float in your mind wherever it feels natural.

Your mind will wander—that's completely normal. When you notice you're no longer thinking your focus word, gently bring your attention back to it. Continue this practice for 10 minutes. When time is up, take a moment to sit quietly before slowly opening your eyes.

Now, close your eyes and after settling in for a moment or two, start thinking your focus word easily and effortlessly, and continue for the next ten minutes.

Reflecting on Your First Meditation

You've just completed your first meditation. Everyone's experience is different—you might have found it surprisingly effortless, or you may have faced some challenges. Both reactions are perfectly normal.

During your session, you might have experienced moments of deep peace interspersed with periods of mental activity. Some people find that their awareness stays on the surface, dwelling on everyday thoughts. Others drift between states of calm and mental chatter. Whatever you experienced is exactly what needed to happen.

For your next session, timing matters. If you meditated in the morning, plan your second session for late afternoon or early evening. If your first meditation was an afternoon or evening session, schedule your next one for the following morning.

Your Second 10-Minute Meditation

Begin by closing your eyes and taking a few natural breaths. Then, start thinking your focus word, allowing it to float gently in your mind. Let the word change on its own—it might become louder or softer, faster or slower, or it may not seem to change at all. There's no need to control it. If you notice it has disappeared, bring it back when you become aware that it's gone.

When your timer signals that your session has ended, keep your eyes closed for another minute or two. You may notice subtle changes in your body and mind—perhaps a sense of calm. Then, gradually open your eyes. Let the world come back into focus naturally as you take a few breaths before getting up.

As you continue your practice, slowly increase the length of your sessions. Start with ten minutes twice daily and work up to 15–20-minute sessions. Listen to your body. If 15 minutes feel too long, scale back your time until you're comfortable again. There's no rush.

How you conclude your meditation is as important as how you start it. Imagine yourself as a diver emerging from the ocean depths—you wouldn't speed straight to the surface.

Allow yourself time to transition. Perhaps wiggle your fingers and toes or stretch gently. Some individuals briefly open their eyes before closing them again, letting their senses adjust gradually. This careful transition helps you integrate the benefits of your practice into daily life. The tranquility you've cultivated during meditation isn't intended to stay where you meditated—it's meant to accompany you into every moment of your day.

Chapter 7: Questions and Answers for New Meditators

These are the questions most frequently asked by new meditators.

Q: I feel so unsure of myself. Am I doing it right?

A: It's perfectly normal to question whether you're meditating correctly. The simplicity of the practice often makes us wonder whether we're missing something essential.

Our minds are conditioned to evaluate and measure progress in everything we do. But meditation operates differently. It's not about achieving a particular state or reaching specific milestones. It's about allowing your natural awareness to unfold without interference.

Think of meditation like watching clouds pass across the sky. You don't try to control their movement or shape—you simply observe. Some days your mind will be stormy, other days clear. Both experiences are equally valid parts of the practice.

The moment you stop trying to force a particular outcome is often when meditation reveals its true nature. If you're sitting quietly and maintaining a gentle awareness of your focus word, you're practicing correctly. Trust in that simplicity.

Q: I've been experiencing many memories coming to mind during my meditation. Is that typical?

A: Yes, memories that come up during meditation are common. Some people recall childhood memories that haven't emerged in decades. Sometimes the recollections are vivid, as if they're reliving the experience rather than simply remembering it.

Q: Sometimes, I see colors, geometric shapes, or landscapes in my mind's eye. Does this have any specific significance?

A: Experiences like these can be engaging, but the instruction remains the same. When you notice you've drifted from the focus word, gently return to it. Also, avoid trying to recreate any experiences. If a pleasant experience happens again, that's wonderful; if it doesn't, that's perfectly fine. Remember, just as each day is experienced differently, every meditation will also be a unique experience.

Q: I felt drowsy during meditation. Is that okay?

A: Absolutely. Feeling sleepy during meditation is common when your body needs rest. Don't resist the drowsiness. If you happen to fall asleep, avoid trying to compensate for lost time by extending your meditation; instead, meditate for a few minutes before resuming your activities. Meditation naps can be very refreshing, and you might feel more alert upon waking up. You may fall asleep during meditation less often or for shorter periods as your body becomes less fatigued.

Q: My mind races constantly when I meditate. Does that mean I'm not meditating correctly?

A: A racing mind doesn't mean you're meditating incorrectly. It's natural for many types of thoughts to occur. Often, these thoughts assist you in mentally processing pressing concerns, allowing you to address them with greater clarity later. Remember, a thought is just a thought, and the way to handle thoughts remains the same: When you notice that a thought has taken the place of your focus word, gently return to your focus word.

Q: What should I do if I have persistent thoughts and find it hard to focus on my word?

A: Thoughts that arise during meditation stem from the natural processes of self-purification, repair, and relaxation within your nervous system, resulting from the deep rest you experience. Sometimes, thoughts can become so persistent or intense that the focus word is difficult to think effortlessly, and other thoughts overshadow it. Instead of resisting this, observe the flow of thoughts without judgment. Typically, a few minutes of gentle observation helps lessen the intensity of thoughts, making it easier for you to return to the focus word.

This more intense release and purification process can continue throughout a meditation or multiple sessions. Gradually, the blockages contributing to the intensity will diminish, allowing you to experience greater tranquility during meditation.

Even if your meditations are filled with thoughts, you will likely notice improvements in how you feel during your daily activities because of your nervous system's ongoing purification and refinement. If you experience exceptionally strong thoughts during meditation, sit comfortably with your eyes closed for a few minutes afterward. Let go of your focus word and give yourself extra time before returning to your regular activity and getting up.

Q: How can I tell if meditation is beneficial for me? Should I evaluate it based on how I feel during the meditation itself?

A: Evaluating the effectiveness of meditation isn't about your subjective experience during the practice. A session in which your mind feels scattered can be just as valuable as one that feels peaceful. While some practitioners report experiencing "flashy" moments during meditation, what truly matters are the benefits that gradually emerge in daily life.

The practice establishes a foundation for greater emotional regulation, stress management, and mental clarity—benefits that may not be immediately apparent during sessions. Rather than judging meditation by momentary feelings, observe its longer-term effects on overall well-being, stress levels, and responses to daily challenges. Regardless of whether your meditation experience feels challenging or unremarkable, it still functions beneath the surface to foster positive changes. The key is to maintain consistent practice while letting go of expectations regarding how each session should feel.

Q: Occasionally, I have brilliant insights and ideas during meditation.

A: Many people experience expansive feelings or what appears to be a profound insight or a brilliant idea during meditation. If these occur, enjoy them.

While meditating, you might think you've come up with a brilliant idea—perhaps a business plan, a solution to a complex problem, or the plot for a novel. Resist the urge to disrupt your meditation session. Instead, jot down your idea as soon as you finish meditating. Later, review your idea and determine if it's worth pursuing. True brilliance will shine just as brightly in the light of day as it does during your meditation.

Q: Sometimes, my thoughts seem pretty urgent.

A: You may experience thoughts during meditation that seem urgent and demand immediate attention. Unless there is danger (like someone getting hurt or if you smell something burning in the kitchen), try to resist the impulse to leave your meditation suddenly. It's just a powerful thought, much like any other intense thought. Handle it as we've discussed before and reintroduce your focus word when your mind has calmed enough for you to easily think the focus word again.

Q: My focus word changed while I was meditating. Is that okay?

A: Absolutely. Your focus word might have become louder or softer. It might have sped up or slowed down. A focus word can slow down so much that it seems to stretch out endlessly. Or it can seem like a faint impulse, almost going by itself in some distant corner of your awareness.

Whatever it does, go with it. Don't try to influence it. If you find the word changing, even becoming almost unrecognizable, allow it to happen.

Some people find that their focus word sometimes disappears, and for a few seconds, their thoughts also stop. This is an experience of pure awareness. While this profound silence can be quite enjoyable, it is not a goal. Individuals who meditate for years may never experience pure awareness, yet they gain as much from meditating as those who do.

You may notice that the mental repetition of your focus word synchronizes with your breathing or heartbeat. Don't try to synchronize it or stop it from synchronizing. Avoid creating or influencing a pattern through your efforts.

Q: I'm experiencing thoughts and my focus word at the same time.

A: It's common to have both thoughts and the focus word simultaneously. The key is to reintroduce the focus word whenever you notice you've lost it. Thoughts may continue alongside it, or the focus word may replace the thoughts; either is fine. However, if you keep pursuing your thoughts without returning to the focus word, despite being aware that you're not thinking it, that's not the correct practice. Correct practice involves returning to the focus word each time you become aware you're not thinking it.

Q: I've experienced some sensations and discomfort during meditation. Is that normal?

A: Yes, experiencing various sensations, even when they cause some discomfort at times, is entirely normal.

Many meditators feel tingling during meditation, while others may experience heaviness in their arms or legs. Some might sense a floating sensation, while others may notice warmth in different parts of their body. Some may also feel numbness in their hands or feet. These often-transient sensations can be neutral, pleasant, or uncomfortable.

The body's release of built-up tension or stress can sometimes lead to discomfort, which usually diminishes by the end of the session.

Although less common, some individuals may experience tightness in their heads, sudden urges to laugh or cry, surges of anger, or feelings of worry or anxiety. These feelings typically fade by the end of the meditation session. Sometimes, tension-release side effects may last throughout a meditation, and less frequently, they might continue between sessions. If the experience feels uncomfortable, sit quietly and scan your body. If you notice any physical sensations anywhere in your body, allow your attention to be with them one at a time for a few moments.

These reactions may persist for several sessions and indicate that stress is being released.

Q: I feel that my breathing is quite shallow.

A: As the mind settles, cellular metabolism, energy consumption, heartbeat, and breathing slow down. This is especially noticeable in our breath. Sometimes, our breath may become so faint that we need to take a deep breath to catch up.

Q: Can I meditate during my commute?

A: For some individuals, commuting to and from work on public transportation is the only opportunity they have to meditate. Some find this easy right away, while others need time to adjust. Regardless of your initial response, meditating successfully during your commute is still possible.

When meditating during your commute, make sure your surroundings are safe. If they are, consider using noise-canceling devices to block out distractions. Don't resist background chatter; with practice, it will feel less intrusive. Based on noise levels, crowding, and stops, identify the best part of your commute for meditation.

Q: Can I learn meditation while bedridden?

A: Meditation can be an excellent companion when bedridden. It provides a profound rest that helps your body heal.

While it's best to learn the basics of meditation when your mind is clear—which means postponing practice if you have a fever or are on short-term medications that make you drowsy—don't let long-term pain medications hold you back. If chronic pain is a part of your daily life and medication helps you manage it, meditation is worth trying. Many people successfully meditate while taking prescribed pain medication.

The goal isn't perfection—it's finding what works for you. Some days, your meditation may feel foggy or unfocused, while on other days, you might experience clarity and calm. Every experience is valid, and each attempt at meditation is worthwhile. Be patient with yourself, and trust that the benefits will unfold in their own time and way.

When you decide to learn, set consistent daily meditation times with friends, family, or hospital staff. Have someone assist with the meditation preparation instructions and arrange your environment as well as possible. For instance, make yourself comfortable by using pillows for support. If possible, elevate the bed to help you stay alert.

Then, when you're ready to begin, watch the "How to Do Kosher Meditation" animation and follow the instructions.

Inform your doctor that you are beginning meditation and share the research from this book regarding the health benefits of meditation, including the potential for reconsidering the need for or adjusting the dosage of some medications. Additionally, please share Appendix B, "Information for Healthcare Providers."

Embrace Your Journey

Welcome to the world of meditation! You've taken your first step on a journey that can bring profound relaxation, increased self-awareness, better health, and a deeper sense of well-being into your life. Meditation requires no special skills or equipment—just a willingness to set aside a few minutes each day to be with yourself in a new way.

Once again, your experience can vary from day to day. Don't worry. Sometimes, your mind may be quieter during certain sessions and more active during others. You might experience days when you feel deeply relaxed and other days when sensations in your body or racing thoughts in your mind dominate your entire session. It's all part of the process.

Most importantly, maintain consistency in the timing and frequency of your practice. Prioritize meditation as you would prioritize brushing your teeth or showering. This remarkably simple self-care tool can yield profound benefits that far outweigh the effort required.

Chapter 8: If Meditation Gets Bumpy: Managing Resistance, Restlessness, Discomfort, and Trauma

Challenges and What to Expect

Meditation provides powerful tools for self-discovery and present-moment awareness. Like any transformative practice, it is important to understand not only its benefits but also its potential challenges.

Timing Your Practice

Most people find that meditating for 15 to 20 minutes twice a day works well. However, remember that this is your practice. Starting with 7- to 10-minute sessions is perfectly fine, and you can gradually extend your meditation time as you become more comfortable.

Understanding Side Effects

Research shows that most people practice meditation without experiencing adverse effects. However, one study found that 8.3% of meditators report adverse experiences, similar to the rates seen in psychotherapy.[1]

Some reported effects include:

- Physical responses like headaches or muscle tension
- Increases in anxiety or emotional sensitivity
- Changes in sleep patterns
- Feelings of detachment
- Fluctuations in mood

Other documented adverse effects include altered perceptions, derealization, delusions, hallucinations, and heightened emotional states. These effects are relatively uncommon and are more frequently reported among individuals who have pre-existing mental health conditions.[2]

What Causes These Effects?

Many meditation teachers attribute side effects to either the release of stored tension or incorrect practice—most often, some strain has crept into the meditation. While research doesn't prove this explanation, experience shows that many physical discomforts can be alleviated by reviewing how to meditate effortlessly.

Taking Control of Your Practice

You are always in control of your meditation journey. If you feel ongoing discomfort, you can:

- Reduce your session length,

- Review the "how to meditate" instructions and watch the animation, or
- Take a break and start again when you're ready.

Many people find meditation transformative, but others may decide it's not for them. Adjust or pause your practice as needed. Meditation should serve your well-being, not compromise it.

Remember, it's fine to step back or stop altogether. Your meditation practice should adapt to your life, not the other way around. Many individuals discover their optimal balance with shorter sessions or other practices that better align with their personality and goals.

Dealing with Restlessness

Feeling restless and calm at different times during the same meditation is normal. Restlessness arises as the body resolves accumulated stresses, which is part of the healing process.

If you often feel restless or uneasy during a 15- to 20-minute meditation, consider shortening the time until you find what works best for you. Experiment to discover a time length that allows you to settle in, at least for part of your meditation. As you continue to meditate and the accumulated tension and anxiety begin to release, you will notice that you feel more relaxed. At that point, you can gradually increase your meditation time again.

When Restlessness Interferes with Effortlessness

If restlessness overwhelms your ability to think your word, it may indicate that your body is releasing deeper tensions due to profound relaxation. If this occurs, begin by scanning your body from your toes and slowly work your way upward. Gradually and intentionally shift your attention upward. Allow your awareness to gently linger on any area where you feel a physical sensation or discomfort. Simply be present with these sensations, no matter how mild or subtle they may be. Notice them—don't resist.

You may become aware of several sensations at the same time. Gently allow your awareness to rest on one sensation at a time. As one sensation relaxes, shift your focus to the next. Continue this process until you feel more relaxed and at ease. This indicates that it's time to reintroduce the focus word. Remember, the goal isn't to force relaxation but to let your body balance and heal.

During times of restlessness, your mind may be crowded with thoughts. Don't push them away. When your mind settles, gently return to your focus word. Simply favor your focus word without forcing it over your thoughts.

Take It As It Comes

Some days, you might feel more relaxed than others, and that's completely normal. Sometimes, the mind isn't ready to settle down; it may take another session or two before it feels settled.

As long as you meditate effortlessly and gently return to your focus word whenever you realize you've stopped thinking it, there is no right or wrong. There's nothing to judge. Even if your entire meditation is filled with thoughts, that meditation is perfectly valid.

When you meditate, your mind and body will take what they need at that moment. If you feel tired, you might fall asleep, as that's what your body needs most at that time. You're likely to feel refreshed when you wake up.

How to Manage High-Stress Levels

Meditation provides numerous benefits, but it's essential to maintain realistic expectations. This section examines practical ways to incorporate meditation into your routine when stress levels are high.

Imagine facing a significant work deadline or a family emergency. Perhaps someone close to you is sick. The pressure is mounting, and you're feeling anxious. A midday meditation session could help you reset and continue moving forward in these situations. However, avoid making extra sessions a regular habit. Once the stress eases, return to your usual schedule.

Many people who have meditated for years tend to understand their stress patterns. They might notice signs such as tightness in their necks or shoulders or the onset of a headache. When these early warning signs appear, occasionally adding ten minutes to your meditation can help reset your system.

What to Do If You Feel Panicky While Meditating

Imagine being trapped in an elevator. Your heart races, your palms sweat, and a wave of dread washes over you. Now, picture yourself experiencing these same overwhelming emotions during what should be a peaceful meditation session. While it might seem counterintuitive, this situation is more common than you think.

Some individuals, particularly those with pre-existing anxiety, may experience a phenomenon known as "relaxation-induced anxiety" during meditation. This paradoxical response can manifest as a sudden increase in anxiety, muscle tension, or intrusive anxious thoughts and images when a person attempts to relax.[3] It occurs when the mind resists entering a calmer state, sometimes due to a fear of losing control or triggering a flashback to a highly stressful experience.

Suggestions for Managing Panic During Meditation
The 5-5-5 technique.

- Stop and breathe in for five seconds, hold for five seconds, and exhale for five seconds.

Ground yourself.

- Open your eyes right away.
- Next, identify five things you can see, hear, and touch in your surroundings to ground yourself in the present moment.
- Feel your feet touching the floor.
- Notice sensations by briefly scanning your body.
- Keep your attention on each sensation individually until it diminishes or resolves itself.

When to Take a Break

If meditation increases your anxiety or triggers panic attacks, reduce your practice time or pause completely. The goal is to reduce stress, not create it.

Consider alternatives like gentle stretching, breathing exercises, or walking outdoors. A mental health professional may be able to suggest a meditation approach that works for you.

Remember: meditation should support your well-being. Modifying or pausing your practice until you discover what works is perfectly fine. The goal is calmness, but not at any cost.

The Nature of Trauma and Its Complex Relationship with Meditation

Trauma fundamentally differs from ordinary stress due to its overwhelming nature. While we can typically manage daily stressors using various coping mechanisms, traumatic experiences—assault, sexual abuse, natural disasters, war, or sudden loss—can leave us feeling utterly helpless. When fighting or fleeing isn't an option, we freeze, trapping defensive energy within our nervous system.

Understanding the Meditation-Trauma Dynamic

The intersection of meditation and trauma presents a complex landscape. In quiet moments of meditation, trauma survivors may sometimes confront an unsettling paradox: the stillness intended to bring peace can create a void when traumatic memories and flashbacks surface unexpectedly. This happens because meditation removes the everyday distractions that typically help those affected by trauma manage their responses.

According to a study reported in clinical findings by PACEs Connection, meditation can "lead people to some dark places, triggering trauma or leaving individuals feeling disoriented."[4] These effects are more pronounced in those with trauma histories or existing mental health issues, and some practitioners experience increased emotional distress instead of the intended therapeutic benefits.

However, meditation is not inherently unsuitable for trauma survivors. When included in a comprehensive treatment plan, it can provide valuable healing benefits similar to trauma exposure therapies like cognitive behavioral therapy.[5] The key lies in ensuring appropriate support.

Practical Guidelines for Safe Practice

Seek Professional Support

Partner with qualified, trauma-informed instructors who understand your unique needs. Keep an open dialogue with healthcare providers to ensure proper guidance throughout your practice. Mental health professionals specializing in trauma can assist in developing personalized meditation strategies that respect your limitations and encourage healing.

Start Small and Build Gradually

Begin with short sessions and gradually extend the duration and frequency as you feel comfortable. Pay close attention to your body's signals and reactions. Remember that ease is essential—avoid forcing or straining. Consider shorter sessions or take breaks if discomfort arises until the symptoms lessen.

Embrace Individual Differences

What heals one person may trigger another. Success in meditation for trauma survivors depends on finding the right approach for their unique circumstances. Some may benefit from shorter sessions, while others might favor guided practices or alternative meditation methods that offer greater support.

Beyond Meditation: The Promise of Somatic Experiencing

Understanding Trauma and the Path to Healing

In her book *Beyond the Trauma Vortex into the Healing Vortex*, trauma specialist Gina Ross presents many insights into trauma healing. At the core of her approach lies Somatic Experiencing (SE), a therapeutic method developed by Dr. Peter Levine. While SE was created for therapists, it has evolved into a self-help tool for stress release and mind-body rebalancing, with a public-friendly version called EmotionAid.[6]

Trauma vs. Ordinary Stress

Before exploring healing methods, it's essential to differentiate between ordinary stress and trauma. With everyday stress, we typically believe we can take steps to improve our situation, often through practices like meditation or various coping strategies. Trauma, on the other hand, arises from situations where we feel completely helpless—usually unexpected events beyond our control, such as assault, rape, war, abuse, natural disasters, or the loss of a loved one. When we cannot fight or flee, we freeze, causing the energy intended for defensive action to become trapped in our nervous system.

The Impact of Trapped Trauma

This trapped energy can manifest in various ways. Some individuals may experience flashbacks or nightmares, while others develop intense hypervigilance and a constant sense of danger. Situations resembling the original trauma can trigger similar feelings of helplessness and a loss of control. The weight of trapped trauma often results in a series of physical and mental health issues, especially when exacerbated by feelings of guilt and shame.

The Healing Power of Somatic Experiencing

Somatic Experiencing offers a distinct approach to trauma resolution by focusing on internal bodily sensations and releasing trapped survival energy. The primary tool of this method is the Felt Sense, which uses our awareness to connect with the physical experiences of the present moment rather than our thoughts. This approach recognizes that traumatic stress often manifests as physical sensations in the body. A significant advantage over meditation is that the Felt Sense bypasses the mind; as a result, flashbacks may be significantly reduced.

The process involves carefully scanning the body to identify sensations, even subtle ones, and maintaining attention on each sensation until it naturally resolves. When multiple sensations are noticed simultaneously, it's essential to release them one at a time before moving on to another sensation.

Signs of Healing and Release

As the body begins to release stored trauma, several physical and emotional signs may emerge.

Physical signs may include:

- Yawning and sighing
- Deep diaphragmatic breathing
- Heat waves or warm sweating
- Watery eyes or running nose
- Physical relaxation, particularly in the shoulders
- Decreased blood pressure
- Trembling or shaking
- Stomach gurgling

Emotional signs may include:

- Increased interest in relationships
- Emotional release through crying
- Growing sense of calm and ease

Integrating Different Healing Approaches

Both meditation and Somatic Experiencing aim to gently release chronic stress and trauma. These approaches can complement each other: when meditation reveals uncomfortable trapped energy, EmotionAid techniques can assist in discharging these sensations before returning to the meditation.

During this process, you may experience moments of restlessness or increased mental activity. Instead of resisting these feelings, observe the sensations that arise and release each one individually using the EmotionAid technique. When you feel comfortable, you can resume meditation.

The Role of Professional Support

While self-help techniques such as meditation and EmotionAid can be valuable tools for healing, they should not replace professional treatment for severe trauma. Many traumatic memories and emotions may be too overwhelming to manage alone. This is especially true for individuals diagnosed with post-traumatic stress disorder (PTSD) or certain psychiatric conditions. A qualified therapist can evaluate your needs and assist you in safely incorporating mind-body practices into your healing journey.

While more research is needed, Somatic Experiencing/ EmotionAid and meditation likely complement each other, potentially accelerating the healing process and possibly enhancing outcomes beyond what each method could achieve independently.

Remember that healing from trauma is a gradual process that requires patience and self-compassion. Each person's journey is unique, and there is no universal timeline for recovery. The key is to be gentle with yourself while consistently practicing your chosen healing methods under appropriate professional guidance.

What to Do If It's Not Working

Patience is essential. While many people notice benefits within a few days or weeks, others may take up to four months to see changes. The effects of meditation typically unfold gradually, developing steadily before they become evident. If you follow the basic guidance and feel physically stable, maintain your practice.

Meditation benefits most practitioners, but like any practice, it isn't universal. If you feel worse after a few weeks (even after using the suggested techniques for managing challenges), it may sometimes help to take a break for a few weeks and try again.

Most difficulties arise from extending the duration or frequency of meditation beyond recommended guidelines. However, side effects can occur even when following instructions carefully, including during the initial sessions. Pay close attention to your reactions. If discomfort becomes significant, pause your practice or consult a healthcare provider.

Make It Your Own

Instead of adhering to rigid formulas or pursuing an ideal routine, cultivate a sustainable practice that integrates into your daily life. Whether you choose five minutes or twenty, meditate indoors or outdoors, alone or while commuting, the primary goal remains to establish regular periods of deep relaxation that alleviate accumulated stress and foster healing and inner peace.

Chapter 9:
The Critical Role of Belief in Healing

So far, we have explored the mind's remarkable ability to influence our physical well-being through a simple mental practice that triggers a relaxation response to counteract the effects of stress. Later, in Chapter 12, we will look at how the relaxation response affects a wide range of illnesses where stress is either a cause or significantly complicates treatment.

The Lubavitcher Rebbe maintained that belief in one's healing ability and a positive outlook are essential to health and healing. The following three chapters will explore these connections through different yet interconnected lenses. We will start by examining how our beliefs shape our health outcomes. Then, we will discover how positive thinking can open new avenues or unblock existing ones for healing. Lastly, we will describe how these approaches build resilience.

These chapters will showcase how the Rebbe's advice to thousands who sought his blessings and guidance anticipated many therapeutic practices used today by mental health professionals.

The Science of Belief

In the mid-1800s, Harvard Medical School professor Oliver Wendell Holmes (not to be confused with his son, the Supreme Court Justice) explored the role of belief and expectation in healing. He argued that even scientifically questionable treatments could benefit patients who believed in them.[1] Dr. Benson's research on the relaxation response later confirmed Holmes's findings, demonstrating the remarkable healing capacity of the mind.

Types of Beliefs

Scientific expectation stems from accepting empirical research that demonstrates the mind's influence over the body.[2] This evidence-based approach relies on documented effects of medical interventions on physical health.

Spiritual belief includes faith-based traditions that recognize the existence and influence of a higher power in one's life. Although it is not scientifically measurable, studies indicate that individuals participating in spiritual practices often experience lower stress levels and improved overall health. The Benson-Henry Institute found that utilizing focus words associated with one's belief system enhances healing potential.[3]

Placebos and Nocebos: The Impact of the Mind on Our Health

The relationship between the medical community and the placebo effect has been complex. While many physicians dismissed improvements from placebos as purely psychological, Benson took a different approach. His research demonstrated that the relaxation response outperformed placebos, but instead of disregarding the placebo effect, he acknowledged its therapeutic value.

In 1996, Benson published research showing that placebos benefited 60%–90% of patients with various conditions, including angina, asthma, and ulcers. Success depended on positive beliefs from the patient and the provider and a strong relationship between them.[4]

The Science Behind the Placebo Effect

While the exact mechanisms remain unclear, researchers believe placebos stimulate endorphins, serotonin, and dopamine release.

In a 2022 article for Harvard Health, Matthew Solan reports on groundbreaking research conducted by Ted Kaptchuk, the director of the Program in Placebo Studies & Therapeutic Encounter (PiPS) at the Harvard-affiliated Beth Israel Deaconess Medical Center. Kaptchuk's work explores how the mind and body interact to produce the placebo effect.

Kaptchuk has demonstrated that the interaction between the brain and body leads to measurable health improvements. However, he emphasizes that while placebos can reduce pain and ease treatment side effects, they are not cures. Kaptchuk believes that the ritualistic aspects of treatment may have a more significant impact than previously recognized. He writes, "People associate the routine of taking medicine with a positive healing effect. Even when they know no medicine is involved, the act can stimulate the brain to perceive that healing is occurring."[5]

Recent research supports Kaptchuk's challenge to the conventional wisdom that placebos require deception. Open-label studies, where patients are aware they are receiving placebos, show promising results. A 2021 study in the journal *Pain* found that participants with moderate to severe irritable bowel syndrome (IBS) symptoms who were knowingly taking placebos reported similar symptom improvements as those on conventional medication.[6]

Dr. Lissa Rankin's research, documented in *Mind Over Medicine*, provides compelling evidence of placebo effectiveness:[7]

- Almost 50% of asthma patients reported relief from using a placebo inhaler or sham acupuncture.
- Around 40% of headache sufferers found relief with the help of a placebo.
- Around 50% of colitis patients reported improvement after receiving a placebo treatment.
- Over 50% of individuals experiencing ulcer pain reported significantly reduced discomfort after receiving a placebo.

- A sham acupuncture treatment reduced hot flashes by nearly half, yielding better results than its genuine counterpart.
- As many as 40% of infertility patients showed improvement while taking a placebo "fertility drug."

When it comes to pain management effectiveness, placebos are comparable to morphine. Many studies have demonstrated that most antidepressant medication effects can be linked to the placebo effect.[8]

Placebos vs. Standard Medical Treatments

According to Rankin, research studies may underestimate the effectiveness of placebos. Pharmaceutical companies fund significant medical research, and their methods can bias results against placebos. For instance, they may exclude "excessive placebo responders" and impose "washout phases" to eliminate subjects who respond well to inactive pills. The stakes are high. Considering the multi-billion-dollar profit potential of a new drug, robust placebo performance could threaten a study's ability to demonstrate a drug's superiority.[9]

The Nocebo Effect—The Power of Negative Belief

Excessive focus on illness can induce sickness in people. For example, medical students frequently experience symptoms of diseases they study—a phenomenon known as the nocebo effect, highlighting how negative beliefs can affect health. While placebos illustrate the power of positive thinking, nocebos demonstrate the dangers of negative expectations.

The term *nocebo* (Latin for "I shall harm") was introduced to differentiate the harmful effects of negative beliefs from the benefits of placebos. In clinical trials, patients who are informed about potential side effects often experience those effects even when taking sugar pills.[10]

Benson illustrates the nocebo effect through three scenarios:

- A belief or expectation in your mind that something unhealthy will happen to you
- A belief or expectation in the mind of your physician or mentor that a disorder will happen to you
- A negative set of beliefs and expectations that permeates the relationship between you and your healthcare provider[11]

Research demonstrates the power of nocebos. In one study, 30% of patients in the control group lost hair after receiving saline, as they were warned it might be chemotherapy.[12] Another study found that 80% of patients vomited after drinking sugar water when informed it would cause nausea.[13]

Harnessing Mind-Body Healing

Kaptchuk suggests that healthy living practices such as proper nutrition, exercise, and meditation can enhance the placebo effect when individuals believe in their benefits. While regular relaxation practices can improve health outcomes regardless of belief, combining them with positive expectations increases healing potential.

Two primary obstacles hinder mind–body healing: skeptical healthcare professionals who might deter patients due to their limited understanding and resistant patients who question the credibility of these approaches.

Medicine is broadening its perspective beyond a purely reductionist view that addresses illness solely through physical interventions such as drugs and surgery. Although this limited approach remains prevalent, increasing evidence regarding the role of belief in healing is slowly transforming the medical landscape. Embracing the mind–body connection provides a more holistic path to health and recovery.

Chapter 10: Cognitive Restructuring, Reframing, and Positivity

After requesting a joyous song during a farbrengen (Chassidic gathering) about teshuva (return) with joy, the Rebbe stood up and danced. Someone shouted, "Nasha biriyot!"—"We won!" The Rebbe accepted this and added that soldiers going out to war, despite it being a difficult battle, march with a victorious song, giving them strength of heart.

> *The Weekly Farbrengen*
> Merkaz Anash, Issue 793

"Everything can be taken from a man but one thing: the last of the human freedoms—to choose one's attitude in any given set of circumstances, to choose one's own way."

> Victor Frankl, *Man's Search for Meaning*

Understanding Cognitive Therapy

Aaron Beck pioneered cognitive restructuring in the 1960s, introducing a method to transform negative thinking patterns into constructive ones. His foundational insight was both simple and profound: our thoughts about an event shape our feelings and behaviors more than the events themselves.

While working with patients who suffered from depression, Beck recognized patterns of irrational thinking that he called "cognitive distortions." These distortions included exaggerated negative interpretations and persistent feelings of hopelessness. His insights led to the creation of cognitive therapy, which he described in his seminal work "Cognitive Therapy for Depression." This approach demonstrated effectiveness through clinical research and expanded to treat various disorders, including bipolar disorder, schizophrenia, PTSD, and anxiety.[1]

The Process of Mental Restructuring

Cognitive restructuring begins with self-awareness. The first essential step is recognizing automatic thoughts—those involuntary responses triggered by situations that frequently provoke anxiety or guilt. These thoughts aren't random; they arise from deep-seated beliefs about ourselves, others, and the future.

One pattern is catastrophizing—assuming the worst possible outcome, often with minimal evidence. While occasional pessimism is normal, some individuals transform minor setbacks into perceived disasters, leading to increased anxiety and depression. Fortunately, those who instinctively exaggerate the severity of minor issues can learn to better manage their pessimistic thoughts by recognizing and restructuring or reframing their amplified conclusions.

The restructuring process involves three key steps:

1. Identifying negative thought patterns
2. Evaluating the evidence that supports these ideas
3. Reframing outcomes with realistic and balanced alternatives

This approach helps manage anxiety and depression while enhancing self-worth and relationships through more balanced perspectives.

The Jewish Perspective on Positive Thinking

Judaism has addressed these issues over the millennia, particularly the role of *bitachon* (trust) and *emunah* (faith) in Jewish life. Rabbi Tzvi Freeman provides an insightful perspective on bitachon, and the following discussion draws from his writings on this topic.[2]

Bitachon is an optimistic outlook rooted in emunah, the belief that G-d is in control and that He loves us, wanting only what is good for us. In Rabbi Freeman's words:

> The person who holds such an attitude will always be able to point out the positive side of life's experiences, but it's obvious that his

or her bitachon is not based upon these. It is not an attitude based on experience, but one that creates experience. It says, "Things will be good because I believe they are good."

On the other hand, bitachon is not a strategy to manipulate the universe. Your belief does not create goodness; the good in which you have such confidence is already the underlying reality. Your belief only provides the means for that reality to emerge.

Those who incorporate bitachon and emunah as core aspects of their being consistently identify the silver lining in life's ups and downs. They naturally embody the positivity described in this chapter. Always seeing the cup as half full is a profound blessing.

For the rest of us, cultivating bitachon requires significant effort. At times, when someone needed to develop more trust, the Rebbe recommended studying *Shaar Habitachon* (Gate of Trust), written in the eleventh century by Rabbi Bachya ibn Pekuda, even a few times.[3]

Many Jews and non-Jews alike know the story of Rabbi Akiva (50 AD–135 AD) and the fox, a preeminent example of positivity.

The Midrash recounts that four Jewish sages traveled to Jerusalem. Upon arriving at Mt. Scopus, they tore their garments in response to the sight of the Holy Temple's destruction. When they reached the Temple Mount, they saw a fox emerge from the place of the Holy of Holies.

Witnessing the complete desecration, the first three wept, while Rabbi Akiva laughed.

Perplexed, they said, "Akiva, why are you laughing?"

He responded, "Why are you weeping?"

They said, "A place [so holy] that it is said of it, 'the stranger that approaches it shall die,' and now foxes traverse it, and we shouldn't weep?"

Rabbi Akiva answered by recalling two prophecies about the Temple. Uriah, who lived during the First Temple, prophesied that Zion would be plowed like a field and Jerusalem would lie in ruins. Zechariah, who lived during the Second Temple, prophesied that old men and women would yet sit in the streets of Jerusalem. Connecting the two, Rabbi Akiva concluded that as long as Uriah's prophecy remained unfulfilled, he feared that Zechariah's prophecy might not come true. With Uriah's prophecy at last fulfilled, Zechariah's prophecy became a certainty.

After hearing his explanation, they responded, "Akiva, you have consoled us! Akiva, you have eased our hearts!"

The Baal Shem Tov (1698–1760) was one of the first rabbis to emphasize the importance of joy in Jewish practice. Following the Chmielnicki massacres in the 1600s in Ukraine, he recognized that healing required both physical and spiritual approaches. Healing the spirit involved serving G-d with joy; a revolutionary idea for that era.

The Lubavitcher Rebbe was a master of cognitive restructuring, reframing, and positivity. Among his many teachings, maintaining a positive outlook in the face of seemingly insurmountable difficulties stands out as a timeless principle that captures his profound insights into human psychology and spiritual growth. The Rebbe's belief in the power of positivity and its transformative potential has made a tremendous impact.

In his book *The Positivity Bias: Practical Wisdom for Positive Living*, Rabbi Mendel Kalmenson examines the Rebbe's lifelong aspiration that people appreciate and focus on the many blessings in their lives rather than the opposite. He explores why positivity was crucial to the Rebbe and provides examples of how this approach proved life-changing for those seeking his guidance.[4]

The Rebbe consistently encouraged individuals to focus on the positive despite negativity or adversity. For him, denying negativity wasn't an escapist ideology but a matter of survival. The Russian Revolution in 1917 brought brutal efforts to undermine Jewish observance through murder, imprisonment, torture, and exile. Both of his parents were exiled to Siberia, where his father died after enduring immense suffering. Later, in Europe, he lived through the Holocaust and witnessed the depths of human depravity. Nevertheless, he remained optimistic, providing spiritual guidance and hope to his followers.

Rabbi Kalmenson writes:

> In a rare personal disclosure to one of his Chasidim and a trusted confidante, R. Berel Junik, the Rebbe once alluded to his focus on seeing things positively stems from his harrowing past, saying, "I worked on myself to always look at things in a positive light; otherwise, I could not have survived."[5]

Kalmenson continues:

> This deceptively simple statement encapsulates the book's basic premise: living a life of positivity is a choice, not a circumstance, and it derives from perspective, not personality. It is not the events of our lives that shape us but the meanings we assign to those events. In other words, if you change how you look at things, the things you look at change.[6]

Spiritually speaking, a positive approach to life is grounded in the belief that every individual, event, and element has a divine purpose and is inherently good. Although challenging, focusing on this inherent goodness aligns us with the divine purpose of creation, promoting personal growth and spiritual fulfillment.

Recent neuroscience research highlights the transformative impact of words on brain function. Rabbi Kalmenson summarizes studies by Andrew Newberg, M.D., and Mark Robert Waldman, suggesting that a single word can affect gene regulation and stress responses. Their MRI scans demonstrate that negative words increase activity in the amygdala, the brain's fear center, and even short exposure to negative words can heighten anxiety or depression.[7]

Conversely, positive words have a positive impact on various brain regions, especially the parietal and frontal lobes. Maintaining a focus on positivity leads to structural changes in the thalamus, ultimately affecting how individuals perceive themselves and their environment.

The Rebbe viewed positivity as a catalyst for social change and believed that individuals could motivate others through their positive actions. His philosophy led to the development of the Chabad-Lubavitch movement's outreach programs, which continue to impact communities around the globe.

The Rebbe's concept of positivity is not about denial but about perception—acknowledging the negative while choosing to focus on the positive. Decades before these concepts became part of psychological terminology, he had already applied reframing and restructuring with thousands who sought his guidance. This approach can help anyone, regardless of faith or cultural background, cope with personal adversities and societal challenges.

> "Tracht gut vet zein gut." (Think good and it will be good.)

This was one of the Rebbe's most common messages to those seeking counsel. More than merely offering hope, the Rebbe conveyed that maintaining a positive outlook could transform a potentially harmful outcome into a favorable one by remaining open to positive results.

Words Make a Difference

The Rebbe's speech showcased his careful choice of uplifting words and phrases. In *The Positivity Bias*, Rabbi Kalmenson emphasizes the Rebbe's language preferences: *due date* versus deadline, *the opposite of love* versus hate, *the opposite of truth* versus lying, *the opposite of blessings* versus curses, *the opposite of humility* versus arrogance, *the opposite of joy* versus sadness, and *the opposite of life* versus death.

A close friend once told the Rebbe he was in the *shamata* (Yiddish for clothes) business. The Rebbe countered that he was in the clothing business. He strongly recommended *beit refuah*, meaning "house of healing," over the Israeli term *beit cholim*, meaning "house of the sick," for hospitals to emphasize a focus on recovery.

Selections from *The Positivity Bias: Practical Wisdom for Positive Living*, by Rabbi Kalmenson.

G-d's Love Is Unconditional

During the Yom Kippur War in 1973, a sergeant in the Israel Defense Forces (IDF) recounted how his Special Forces unit faced overwhelming Egyptian forces. His unit's fortifications served as the only barrier between the Egyptians and Tel Aviv. One soldier, holding a book of

Tehillim (Psalms), encouraged them to place their trust in prayer.

The sergeant, feeling faith for the first time, made a vow: "Master of the world, if we make it out of this hellhole alive, I promise to wear tefillin (small black leather boxes containing Torah verses that Jewish men wear during weekday morning prayers) for the rest of my life!"

After miraculously repelling the Egyptians, he received the Israel Hero Medal, the nation's highest honor for valor. However, he lost his left arm, which he would have used to wear tefillin. With his faith shaken, he sought answers from several rabbis but found none that satisfied him.

Everything changed after the sergeant met the Rebbe late one night. Through tears, the Rebbe offered a perspective that transformed his life: "Perhaps this is G-d's way of telling you that His relationship with you is unconditional. He loves you not for what you may or may not do, but simply for who you are, like a parent loves a child."

Thank You

Another IDF soldier lost both of his legs to a landmine in the Golan Heights. Despite being honored as a national hero, he encountered difficulties in social interactions and daily activities. In 1976, he took part in an Israel Defense Forces (IDF)-sponsored tour to America, where he met the Rebbe in Brooklyn alongside other severely injured veterans.

In his address, the Rebbe gently yet powerfully told the group that losing a limb or faculty inherently indicates that G-d has given the person's soul unique powers to overcome their limitations and exceed the achievements of ordinary people.

The Rebbe explained that this was true regardless of how severe their injuries were. His overarching message was that they were not "disabled" but rather "special" and "unique."

The soldier recalled:

> As he said goodbye, he gave each of us a dollar bill and explained that we should donate it to charity on his behalf, making us partners in fulfilling a mitzvah. He then moved from wheelchair to wheelchair, shaking our hands, handing each of us a dollar, and sharing a personal word or two.
>
> When it was my turn, I saw his face up close and felt like a child. He gazed deeply into my eyes, took my hand in his, pressed it firmly, and said, "Thank you," with a slight nod of his head.
>
> I later discovered that he had told each of us something different. To me, he said, "Thank you." Somehow, he knew that this was exactly what I needed to hear. With those two words, the Rebbe erased all the bitterness and despair that had built up in my heart. I

brought the Rebbe's "Thank you" back to Israel and carry it with me to this very day.

The Rebbe believed that G-d never presents challenges that individuals cannot handle. He viewed injured soldiers not as diminished, but as transformed individuals with unique abilities to inspire change and turn obstacles into opportunities.

The Rebbe concluded with a smile: "I therefore suggest—of course, it's none of my business, but Jews are known for sharing opinions on matters that don't concern them—that you should no longer be referred to as Nechei Yisrael ('the Disabled of Israel,' their official designation by the IDF) but rather as Metzuyanei Yisrael, 'the Exceptional of Israel.'"

Losing Money

A rabbi once expressed his disappointment to the Rebbe regarding an unpaid loan to a friend. The Rebbe explained that when a monetary loss is unavoidable, it may occur due to misfortune or as an act of kindness. This new perspective prompted the rabbi to conclude, "Rather than losing money with tears, I can lose it with a smile."

Guinea Pig or Pioneer?

When a 14-year-old girl resisted attending a new Lubavitch high school, she wrote to the Rebbe, defiantly concluding, "I do not want to be a guinea pig." The Rebbe's reply simply crossed out "guinea pig" and replaced it with "chalutzah" (pioneer). This single-word transformation ignited her spirit: "Chalutzah? You're encouraging me to be a pioneer? I'll ascend the mountain, I'll cross the river, I'll do anything!"

The message resonated with her independent spirit. A single word encapsulated her desire to be unique, extraordinary, and different while breaking new ground. Embracing her role as a trailblazer, she enrolled in the new school and became part of the first "pioneer" class. Her decision fostered a lifelong relationship with the school, culminating in her appointment as its principal years later. By changing just one word, the Rebbe redirected her life's path.

As Rabbi Kalmenson concluded, the Rebbe had an extraordinary ability to turn perceived deficits into unique advantages, talents, and opportunities for personal growth that surpassed what the individuals or others thought possible. When addressing personal impairments or those others face, our perceptions and views can reinforce a fixed set of limitations or uncover previously unknown capabilities. Rather than focusing on difficulties or obstacles, we can choose to recognize the positive and distinct potential in everyone, including ourselves, regardless of the circumstances.

Rabbi Manis Friedman

In his book, *When Bad Things Happen to Good People* (1981), Rabbi Harold Kushner asks why a good and loving G-d would permit suffering and pain. He proposes that G-d is benevolent but not all-powerful in preventing all the evil in the world.

Rabbi Friedman offered a different perspective: Everything G-d does is good, but sometimes we need a broader view to recognize it. He shared the story of a man who missed a flight and a crucial meeting due to traffic. Later, he learned that the plane had crashed and, in that instant, one of the worst days of his life transformed into the best—because he missed that flight.

Rabbi Friedman also addressed the common belief that Jewish suffering surpasses that of other nations, noting that centuries of continuous Jewish existence make comparisons with other nations meaningless, as the vast majority of them have ceased to exist.

Rabbi Avraham Zajac

Rabbi Avraham Zajac, co-founder of SOLA (Chabad-Lubavitch of South La Cienega in Los Angeles), is a Torah scholar known for his caring and compassionate nature. Alongside his wife, Stery, he served as an assistant rabbi at Chabad of Hong Kong, where he had a profound experience.

The story centers around planning a celebration to welcome a new Torah into their synagogue, located in the Hilton Hotel. The occasion united Hong Kong's diverse Jewish communities, with the city agreeing to halt traffic so the crowd could dance with the Torah from the head rabbi's home to the hotel. Inside, Hakafos (dancing with the Torah) and a grand banquet awaited.

The sky was clear as they gathered in the bustling heart of downtown Hong Kong. However, as they danced with the new Torah in the street, a sudden typhoon interrupted the celebration, soaking the crowd and sending most attendees rushing for cover. Rabbi Zajac questioned the timing—after all their effort and unity, couldn't the heavens have waited just a few more minutes? Then, everyone would have already been inside.

His answer came unexpectedly. A voice called out, asking for anyone who spoke Portuguese. Rabbi Zajac spoke Portuguese and approached a soaked, emotional middle-aged man who began dancing around the Bima in the empty Shul, crying that "the rain was from G-d!"

The man had been on the Peak Tram, a popular tourist attraction. When the storm hit, he turned back and noticed the celebration below—a Torah being danced with in the street and Jewish music playing. After a year of traveling the world without encountering anything Jewish, this sight made him think Mashiach (the Messiah) had arrived. It shook him to his core.

For Rabbi Zajac, this encounter brought a profound realization. The storm that disrupted their celebration served a Divine purpose. Perhaps in G-d's calculation, connecting one more Jew mattered more than gathering many Jews for the celebration, even one welcoming a new Torah. For Rabbi Zajac, what initially seemed unfortunate was actually a blessing—a reminder that when something appears negative, it's possible we haven't yet seen the end of the story.

Sounds Good. How Do I Do It?

As shared earlier in this chapter, the Rebbe provided a simple answer when asked about maintaining his remarkable optimism: "I worked on myself to always look at things in a positive light."

The Rebbe didn't suggest that positivity comes naturally or is a gift bestowed upon a select few. Instead, he emphasized that it requires conscious effort—he "worked" on himself. This transformational process isn't instantaneous, but a practice cultivated over time, much like building muscle.

While we cannot change events, we can choose how we interpret them. This isn't simply positive thinking or a denial of reality. Instead, it involves developing a deeper understanding of how we perceive and process our experiences. When faced with challenges, we often default to negative interpretations—seeing obstacles instead of opportunities and focusing on what we lack rather than what we have.

Building bitachon (trust) and emunah (faith) enhances our resilience in facing life's challenges. Bitachon isn't just passive trust; it's a catalyst that shapes how we interact with the world. When we genuinely internalize that everything comes from a source of infinite wisdom and kindness, even difficult situations take on new meaning. They contain within them the possibility of transforming into opportunities for growth rather than merely being obstacles to overcome.

While sharing inspirational quotes is easier than developing genuine bitachon, many resources are available to assist. As mentioned, the Rebbe's recommendation to study Shaar Habitachon (Gate of Trust) is particularly relevant. This classic text provides systematic guidance for nurturing authentic trust in Divine Providence, addresses common doubts, and offers practical strategies for reinforcing faith.

Cultivating a positive perspective is like developing any skill—it requires practice and awareness. When confronted with challenges, if our initial reaction leans toward negativity, the key is to learn how to pause and intentionally shift our focus, asking not, "Why is this happening to me?" but rather, "What might this teach me?"

This isn't about forcing cheerfulness or pretending that problems don't exist. It's about what the Bal Shem Tov and other Chassidic masters referred to as ayin tov (a good eye)—the ability to seek out goodness in every situation. Their teaching was straightforward: by looking for the good in others, you cultivate more goodness within yourself and naturally become more aware of it around you.

This perspective encourages individuals to cultivate a positive outlook and recognize the potential for growth and transformation in challenging situations. Consider how frequently past challenges revealed unexpected benefits, such as a job loss that opened the door to a new career.

With consistent practice, this perspective gradually shifts from a conscious effort to an instinctive one. We instinctively recognize the seeds of possibility in each challenge, understanding that what seems to be an obstacle today may be a stepping stone to a better tomorrow.

Chapter 11: Resilience: How to Bounce Back Better

Resilience isn't just about recovering from setbacks—it's about growing stronger through them. When we build resilience, we develop more internal resources to respond to life's challenges, making inevitable obstacles more manageable.

Beyond Homeostasis: Adaptation in Action

Our bodies maintain balance through homeostasis, keeping everything from temperature to blood pressure in check. Our minds work similarly. But psychological resilience goes further—it's not just about maintaining equilibrium but improving our ability to handle whatever life throws our way. Resilience surpasses simple maintenance by incorporating learning and adaptation. It raises baseline functioning, improves stress tolerance, and boosts the ability to adjust to new situations.

Resilience as a Learned Behavior

Rather than being an inherent trait, building resilience involves learnable behaviors, thoughts, and actions. While developing resilience increases stress tolerance, it does not remove emotional pain or distress during difficult times;

however, it may lessen their impact, allowing quicker healing.

The Impact of Resilience Training on Health Care Utilization

A major study conducted by a prominent academic health network in the U.S. demonstrated the impact of resilience training on healthcare utilization.[1] Participants who completed an eight-session program, which included learning relaxation techniques and other strategies for building resilience, showed an extraordinary 43% reduction in overall healthcare service usage during the one-year test period, with 41.9% fewer doctor visits and a 50.3% decrease in imaging tests and medical procedures, which saw a reduction of 21.4%. Emergency department visits decreased by half, dropping from 3.6 to 1.7 per year.

A 2021 study conducted by Park et al. evaluated the Stress Management and Resiliency Training (SMART) program. The research confirmed that higher resilience correlates with social support, optimism, and effective coping strategies, while lower resilience is associated with anxiety and depression.

Research indicates that our mental state directly impacts our immune system, especially regarding stress. A review of 75 studies conducted over two decades revealed two significant findings: First, chronic stress disrupts the immune system, increasing our vulnerability to infections and inflammatory diseases. Second, mind–body practices can help mitigate these adverse effects.[3]

The evidence is compelling: when we're chronically stressed, our bodies shift into a state that promotes inflammation, potentially leading to many health issues. However, there is hope. Recent meta-analyses published in *JAMA (Journal of the American Medical Association) Psychiatry* confirm that mind–body practices effectively reduce stress and bolster our immune system's capacity to protect us. This research suggests that integrating these practices into routine medical care could help reduce and potentially prevent stress-related immune problems.[4]

Building Resilience: Key Factors

The American Psychological Association (APA) identifies supportive relationships as essential to resilience.[5]

Their recommendations include:

- Developing strong connections and accepting support
- Viewing crises as manageable challenges
- Setting realistic goals and taking proactive steps
- Maintaining perspective and a hopeful outlook
- Engaging in self-care and pursuing personal growth

The Stress Management Framework

The four-step process for managing stress caused by negative thoughts and cognitive distortions from the Benson-Henry Institute includes:

1. Stop: Take a mental break.

2. Breathe: Reduce tension through deep breathing.
3. Reflect on your thought patterns and explore alternative perspectives.
4. Choose suitable responses, whether through problem-solving, acceptance, or seeking help.[6]

A Practical Application

To illustrate the four-step method, consider how you might use it to tackle presentation anxiety. Imagine you are the keynote speaker at a major conference, and 30 minutes before your presentation, you realize you've left out an essential slide in your PowerPoint presentation. To ease your anxiety, you would follow these steps:

- Stop and take a moment to observe signs of panic or anxiety, like a racing heart or rapid breathing.
- Take deep breaths to calm your nervous system and restore your composure.
- Reflect on the situation by reminding yourself, "Forgetting one slide won't ruin the whole presentation. I have prepared well, and I know my material. I can summarize the information on that slide."
- Consider taking constructive action, like telling yourself, "I can improvise on that part, or briefly explain the oversight and provide the information later. I'm capable of adapting to this situation."

By consciously using the stop-breathe-reflect-choose method, you can change your reaction to stress and build resilience. This process helps you break down negative thoughts, promotes a more balanced perspective, and equips you to face challenges with greater composure and effectiveness.

Seeking Help and Moving Forward

The evidence for resilience as a learnable skill that can significantly impact individual well-being and healthcare utilization is compelling. As healthcare systems globally face increasing pressures, implementing evidence-based resilience training programs offers a promising path to enhanced individual outcomes and lower healthcare costs.

As the Rebbe often emphasized, every challenge contains the seed of an opportunity for growth.[7] This perspective aligns perfectly with modern resilience research, suggesting that adversity can become a catalyst for personal development when approached with the right mindset. The Rebbe's teaching that "every descent is for the purpose of an ascent" particularly resonates with our understanding of resilience as a dynamic process that can lead to functioning well beyond baseline levels.[8]

Chapter 12: Mind–Body Techniques May Help Certain Health Conditions

Understanding the Scope and Limitations of Mind–Body Practices

Eliciting the relaxation response can help many people relieve stress while boosting energy and resilience. Moreover, Dr. Benson and others have documented numerous health conditions that have improved or even healed through the relaxation response. This chapter discusses some of those conditions.

Before starting meditation for health reasons, consult your healthcare provider. They should be aware of and monitor your meditation practice, especially since it may impact your current treatments. While meditation can sometimes reduce the need for certain medications, any modifications to your treatment plan should be made under your doctor's guidance.

Share Appendix B with your provider to help evaluate whether meditation is appropriate for you.

Meditation is generally considered safe for most people who limit their practice to 15 to 20 minutes twice daily. However, individuals with specific medical and psychological conditions should consult their healthcare provider before starting.

People experiencing depression or suicidal thoughts should meditate with the support of a mental health professional.

Post-traumatic stress disorder (PTSD): Meditation can trigger flashbacks, so it should be closely monitored by a healthcare professional experienced in treating PTSD. Schizophrenia and psychotic disorders: Meditation may potentially worsen symptoms in some cases. It should be practiced under the guidance of a mental health provider.

Dissociative disorders: Techniques that promote deep relaxation could potentially exacerbate dissociation. It is advisable to proceed with caution and consult a mental health professional.

While meditation may improve some medical conditions, it should not replace medical or psychological treatment when necessary. Individuals with these conditions should consult their healthcare provider before beginning a meditation practice.

Caveat Emptor: The Ongoing Challenge of Evaluating Meditation Research

Navigating Scientific Validity

Many people may pick up this book in search of ways to manage a health condition that they think meditation might help. However, it's essential to understand that meditation is not a cure-all. Many research findings highlighting its benefits are preliminary. It's all too easy to be influenced by claims of effectiveness without actually understanding whether the data supports those claims.

Advocates of various forms of meditation often cite studies to support their claims about effectiveness. Their assertions seem authoritative when research is published in medical and scientific journals. However, it is essential to recognize that publication in a journal does not guarantee reliability. Flawed research—such as poor methodology, investigator bias, and self-serving financial interests—frequently distorts or exaggerates a study's conclusions. Unfortunately, the vast majority of meditation research is permeated by one or more of these flaws.

Bias is particularly concerning when investigators have personal or financial interests in the outcome of a study or when they are strong advocates for the intervention under investigation. Bias can distort the interpretation of study data by exaggerating the significance of positive results or downplaying or neglecting to report adverse outcomes. Whether unintentional or intentional, bias too often leads to claims that go beyond what the data supports.

The challenges in medical, psychological, and behavioral science research are significant and are unlikely to be resolved in the near future. In 2015, Richard Horton, the editor-in-chief of *The Lancet,* one of the world's most prestigious medical journals, wrote:

> The case against science is straightforward: much of the scientific literature, perhaps half, may be untrue. Afflicted by studies with small sample sizes, tiny effects, invalid exploratory analyses, and flagrant conflicts of interest, together with an obsession for pursuing fashionable trends of dubious importance, science has taken a turn towards darkness... In their quest for telling a compelling story, scientists too often sculpt data to fit their preferred theory of the world. Or they retrofit hypotheses to fit their data.[1]

Science and Clinical Experience: A Winning Combination

The cautions don't mean that mind–body techniques can't lead to excellent health outcomes. Although few individual studies meet gold-standard criteria, positive results from hundreds of more or less methodologically challenged studies demonstrate that mind–body interventions deserve serious consideration.

Another reason for greater confidence is the documented reports of clinical encounters that connect health improvements to integrating mind–body methods in treatment plans. Dr. Benson and his colleagues have compiled these reports from Deaconess and Massachusetts General Hospitals, along with additional reports gathered from Harvard Medical School and other institutions [2]

Limited Downside

The mind–body techniques suggested in this book are:

- Easy to learn
- Free or very inexpensive
- Generally effective, with minimal side effects, when practiced as recommended

The Third Leg

Benson's approach to mind–body interventions views them as an integral part of a comprehensive treatment plan. He employs a three-legged stool as a metaphor, emphasizing that surgery, medications, and mind–body approaches (including self-care) are all essential components of treatment that cannot operate independently. Furthermore, relying too heavily on any one leg results in an unsteady stool.[3]

Not a Cure-All, but Significant

Relaxation techniques may not cure most illnesses, but they can assist with some and make others more manageable by potentially reducing the fatigue, anxiety, and depression that often accompany illness. For instance, mind–body techniques may lower blood pressure to safer levels, possibly allowing for a reduced dosage of hypertension medication.[4] Any physician will tell you that this is a win.

"Dis-ease"—A Lack of Ease

Benson's book, *The Relaxation Revolution,* describes how relaxation techniques can improve many health conditions.[5] Contending that all health conditions have a stress component, Benson believes that mind–body approaches can improve virtually every health problem and disease.[6] Research references throughout the book document the impact of eliciting the relaxation response on these conditions. The Benson-Henry Institute for Mind–Body Medicine at Massachusetts General Hospital's website lists over 100 published studies demonstrating the health benefits of mind–body techniques.[7]

The more severe the illness, the greater the stress load on the patient (and the caregiver). Beyond psychological responses such as anxiety and depression, stress can trigger the onset of certain medical conditions. For instance, research on heart attacks and high blood pressure indicates that stress plays a significant role in their etiology.[8]

Synergy

While Benson's mind–body methods can sometimes reduce the debilitating effects of the medical conditions described below, a healthcare professional may suggest combining mind–body techniques with conventional medical interventions, such as medications and surgical procedures.

Conditions Responsive to Mind–Body Therapies

In *The Relaxation Revolution*, Benson lists various conditions that some preliminary studies have reported improving from eliciting the relaxation response, provided that there is a belief and expectation that healing is possible. These conditions include angina pectoris, anxiety, depression, hypertension (high blood pressure), infertility, insomnia, menopause, perimenopause, breast cancer, hot flashes, nausea, general pain, targeted pain (such as abdominal, back, head, joint pain, rheumatoid arthritis, knee, neck, shoulder, or postoperative pain), Parkinson's disease, phobias, premature aging, premature ventricular contractions (extra or skipped heartbeats, palpitations, or heart pounding), and premenstrual syndrome (PMS).[9]

Benson also reports that mind–body approaches can effectively address other medical issues, including allergic skin reactions, bronchial asthma, congestive heart failure, constipation, cough, diabetes mellitus, dizziness, drowsiness, duodenal ulcers, fatigue, herpes simplex (cold sores), hostility and anger, immune problems, impotence, obesity, postoperative swelling, post-traumatic stress disorder (PTSD), and tinnitus (ringing in the ears).[10]

The Relaxation Revolution further focuses on five prevalent medical problems to demonstrate the advantages of mind–body approaches.[11] The following summarizes Benson's research on these conditions.

Hypertension **(Too much tension)**

Benson reports on a study of "isolated systolic hypertension," which affects approximately 10 million Americans, particularly those over 65. The 122 subjects who met the elevated blood pressure criteria and took at least two antihypertensive medications were randomly assigned to one of two groups. One group underwent eight weeks of relaxation training, while the other participated in a lifestyle modification program. Both groups experienced lower blood pressure; however, about two-thirds of the relaxation training group successfully eliminated one of their hypertension medications.[12]

Insomnia

A 1993 Harvard Medical School study explored methods to reduce sleep onset latency (SOL)—the time it takes for people with insomnia to shift from complete wakefulness to sleep. The study divided participants into two groups: one group received stimulus control treatment, while the other underwent a multifactor behavioral intervention incorporating relaxation response techniques. Both groups showed a decrease in SOL, but the multifactor group significantly reduced their average time to fall asleep from 77 minutes to a normal range of 20 minutes.[13]

A 1996 study that employed stimulus control, relaxation response, and behavioral techniques assisted 91% of participants in reducing or eliminating their use of sleep medications while enhancing their sleep quality. [14]

Irregular Heartbeat

A study published in The Lancet demonstrated the effectiveness of a mind–body treatment that utilizes the relaxation response to alleviate irregular heartbeats—premature ventricular contractions (PVCs)—in patients with stable ischemic heart disease, characterized by significant blockage of the arteries leading to the heart, which restricts blood flow and oxygen supply to the heart muscles.

The 11 patients evaluated had stable ischemic heart disease and were not taking any medications for the condition. After four weeks of practicing the relaxation response for 10 to 20 minutes twice daily, eight of the 11 participants experienced a reduced frequency of PVCs.

Since stress can sometimes trigger PVCs and long-term pharmacological therapy is often ineffective, those who experience irregular heartbeats might consider incorporating a mind–body approach into their treatment plan.[15]

Premenstrual Syndrome

Premenstrual syndrome (PMS) is a hormonal condition that affects approximately 75% of women who ovulate, often leading to both physical and emotional symptoms. Physical discomfort may include fatigue, cravings for sweets or salty foods, abdominal bloating and pain, swollen hands or feet, tender breasts, and digestive issues. PMS can also cause depression, irritability, mood swings, and difficulties with concentration and memory. To alleviate PMS symptoms, Dr. Nancy Rigotti suggests lifestyle changes such as incorporating regular aerobic exercise, avoiding caffeine, alcohol, salt, and sweets, and employing stress-reduction techniques like the relaxation response.[16]

A study by Goodale et al., published in *Obstetrics & Gynecology* in 1990, further supports the importance of the relaxation response based on changes observed in a study of 46 women experiencing PMS over five months. Divided into groups, those who practiced the relaxation response showed significantly better results (58%) compared to those who engaged in casual reading (27%) or merely tracked their symptoms (17%). These findings suggest that with consistent practice, the relaxation response may serve as an effective treatment for both physical and emotional premenstrual symptoms, especially those with severe symptoms.[17]

Infertility

According to Alice Domar of the Beth Israel Deaconess Medical Center and Harvard Medical School, infertility treatments often include medications and surgeries, but natural methods should not be overlooked.

In the *Harvard Medical School Family Health Guide*, Domar suggests lifestyle changes such as avoiding alcohol, quitting smoking, and reducing stress to enhance fertility.[18] She cites a study from 1990 that she conducted with Machelle M. Seibel at Harvard Medical School, which included 54 infertile women in a ten-week stress reduction program. Within six months of completing the program, 34% of the women became pregnant, leading to a preliminary finding that stress reduction contributes to treating infertility. The study advises considering behavioral treatments like stress management before or alongside reproductive technologies. [19]

Chapter 13: Non-Kosher Practices

Yoga, mantra meditation, and mindfulness have gained immense popularity worldwide, attracting millions of practitioners. Over a million Jews participate in these practices, often unknowingly engaging in activities that contradict monotheistic beliefs. The following chapters explore some halachic (Jewish law) issues associated with these widespread practices. Understanding the origins and intentions behind these practices is essential for making informed choices.

The Rebbe devoted immense effort to countering the influence of Eastern meditation and yoga, aiming to prevent Jews from becoming involved in Avodah Zarah (idolatry) and being drawn into related cults. These chapters describe his concerns and share his guidance.

As a former Transcendental Meditation (TM) executive who practiced TM and yoga for four hours daily for over a decade, I have witnessed the risks these groups pose from the inside. I know the deliberate deceptions and misinformation at the heart of TM. Unfortunately, many of these same issues also extend to yoga and mindfulness.

As you will discover, TM hides its Hindu origins to attract followers, gain access to public schools and veterans, and secure funding from foundations, the government, and corporations. Celebrities endorse TM because they are led to believe it is simply a relaxation technique; any negative aspects are kept hidden. Meanwhile, most TM teachers accept unreasonably low wages pursuing a hoped-for but ever-elusive promise of enlightenment.

This manipulation poses a particular danger to religious individuals. Misinformation can lead to unintentional participation in Avodah Zarah (idolatry). The following chapters draw heavily from the Rebbe's teachings and my personal experience to help you navigate these complex issues. My goal is to equip you with the knowledge needed to make informed choices.

The Deception Dilemma: When Religious Practices Masquerade as Secular

A critical issue arises when meditation, yoga, and mindfulness practices conceal their religious foundations to appear secular, often for financial gain or proselytization. This dishonesty can mislead unsuspecting individuals seeking stress management into engaging in rituals that clash with their faith.

In 2018, I detailed this issue in my book *Transcendental Deception: Behind the TM Curtain* after discovering that the David Lynch Foundation, serving as a surrogate for TM, was teaching TM to thousands of students in public schools under the pretense of a supposedly secular program called "Quiet Time."[1]

As a former TM teacher, I understood that TM instruction requires the student's participation in a Hindu initiation ritual known as the *puja,* which the instructor chants in Sanskrit. During the ceremony, offerings are made on an altar to various revered Hindu deities and gurus. The meaning of the ceremony was not disclosed to the students, their parents, or school administrators, nor was a translation provided. This lack of transparency is not simply a breach of trust; misrepresenting religious practices as secular has serious consequences.

A Jewish friend learned TM from the CEO of the David Lynch Foundation. Before the instruction, she informed him that she was religious and asked if anything he would teach her might be problematic. He assured her that TM was entirely secular and that he had personally taught hundreds of religious individuals. When he performed the *puja* ceremony, she felt devastated and outraged by the deception.

A retired Army lieutenant colonel was required to learn TM as part of a PTSD treatment program. He was assured it was secular. However, when he sought more information about the ceremony from his TM instructor and program administrators, he faced obstacles at every turn. Feeling as though he had betrayed his Christian faith, he underwent a second baptism to atone for failing what he believed was a test of his faith.

The Need for Transparency

Full disclosure is a basic consumer expectation; lack of transparency lies at the heart of these issues.

- Yoga has deep roots in Hinduism and is practiced as a spiritual discipline by millions of people.
- Many Eastern meditations involve a ceremony honoring a guru or deity, and their mantras are typically linked to Hindu or Buddhist deities.
- Mindfulness-based stress reduction (MBSR), promoted as a secular form of mindfulness, isn't secular. MBSR intentionally obscures its Buddhist origins and beliefs.

All three are steeped in Avodah Zarah (idolatry).

Transparency is essential as meditation and yoga gain popularity in schools and workplaces. Before participating, people have the right to know a practice's origins, goals, and risks. While some are comfortable with exposure to teachings from different religions, others may feel deceived or emotionally distressed upon discovering later that they unwittingly took part in a religious ceremony—especially if it was intentionally concealed. This is especially true for those committed to a different faith. Informed consent is vital to minimize harm.

Chapters 14, 15, and 16 examine the halachic issues related to yoga, mantra meditation, and mindfulness. Although some may argue that these practices have become sufficiently secularized, a closer examination shows this isn't true.

Protecting Yourself: Warning Signs of Dangerous Gurus and Cults

Many people view a cult as a group with unconventional beliefs, where members often dress similarly and live communally. However, cult-like groups exist in various forms and can appeal to anyone. The term refers to a psychological system of control that can arise anywhere.

Cults have existed for thousands of years and grew significantly in the 1960s and 1970s as people began exploring alternative lifestyles and new-age spiritual and religious practices. However, cults did not disappear after the 1970s; they are still widespread today. Thousands exist in the U.S. alone and may or may not be religious or spiritual.

The belief that one must be broken to join these groups is false. When a person undergoes a significant change, such as relocating, starting a new job, or going through a breakup, they enter a vulnerable transition phase. Cults can exploit this by saying, "We are here for you; we have all the answers, and we can help you reach your potential."

No one joins a cult; they join a group they believe will help them understand themselves better, cope with loneliness, or fulfill a desire to make a difference in the world. This is part of why people seek involvement. Group members may tell them how amazing and valued they are, which can lead them to overlook warning signs that something is wrong.

So, what is a cult? It is more beneficial to discuss the system of control rather than the groups themselves. Coercive control often takes place in cults, where a leader employs tactics that frequently harm members' physical, emotional, and/or financial well-being.

Questions are often met with thought-terminating clichés meant to shut down discussions, like "Everything happens for a reason." Frequently, asking questions leads to attempts to control the inquirer by convincing them they are the problem—they need to try harder, pray more, or donate more money.

Other tactics include:

- Labeling outsiders as "others" and either ignoring or vilifying them.
- Love bombing—excessive flattery is a technique used to secure people's loyalty.
- Gaslighting manipulates individuals into doubting their perception of reality.
- Shaming is a powerful tool as well.

Any group can become a cult—whether it's a therapy group, a music class, a yoga class, or an activist group—if the leader is controlling and manipulative. Therefore, it's not about the group's stated purpose or goals; it's about the system and whether it manipulates individuals.

Steven Hassan, Ph.D., an expert on cults and groups of "undue influence," developed the BITE model of authoritarian control. In summary, the BITE model includes the following components.

- **Behavior:** how manipulative groups control and dominate their members' actions through strict rules, rewards, and punishments, restricting individual autonomy.
- **Information:** tactics used by manipulative organizations to control the flow of information through censorship and propaganda, and limit members' access to external perspectives.
- **Thought:** the psychological techniques such groups use to shape beliefs and attitudes, suppress critical thinking, and encourage conformity.
- **Emotion:** how manipulative organizations exploit emotions, creating dependency and loyalty through love-bombing, guilt, and fear-based indoctrination.[2]

To protect yourself from potentially harmful groups or behaviors, stay connected with others, practice active listening, and apply critical thinking. Be aware of efforts to pressure you to disconnect from family, friends, support networks, outside activities, and your savings. Familiarize yourself with coercive control techniques that groups use to attract and retain members. Educate yourself and your family to recognize and resist these groups.

Chapter 14: Yoga

This chapter examines the troubling relationship between yoga and various idolatrous practices. While I am not an expert in yoga or Jewish law, I present what I believe are the most significant issues based on my research and discussions with knowledgeable authorities.

Spiritual dangers run deeper than many practitioners realize, and obtaining reliable information about these matters can be challenging. Even basic facts regarding yoga's origins and spiritual significance are often clouded by contemporary marketing and widespread misconceptions.

For example, many yoga poses are linked to Hindu deities and carry deep spiritual significance for Hindus. In Hinduism, yoga is a path to spiritual liberation and connecting with the divine. The word "yoga" comes from the Sanskrit term "yuj," which means to yoke or unite. Traditionally, Hindus practiced yoga to unite their minds, bodies, and spirits, establishing a connection with their higher selves. Today, many people, including Hindus, primarily use it for exercise.

This chapter explores religious and philosophical considerations and offers carefully vetted suggestions from rabbinic authorities and observant yoga instructors to tackle some of these challenges.

This chapter is intended solely to inform the reader about the issues. The information provided is not a substitute for an authoritative religious ruling, and nothing in this chapter should be interpreted as a heter (religious permission) to practice yoga. Given the significant spiritual implications involved, seeking guidance from a qualified religious authority expert in Jewish law and the specific practices being discussed is crucial.

The Growth of Yoga in the U.S. and Globally

Over the past 20 years, yoga has gained remarkable popularity in the United States and around the globe. A 2016 *Yoga Journal* study estimated 36 million yoga practitioners in the U.S. alone. This marks a significant increase from the 20 million practitioners reported in a similar survey conducted in 2012. In 2016, about 80 million Americans, or 34%, stated they were somewhat or very likely to practice yoga in the next 12 months.[1] With an estimated six to ten million Jews in the United States and another seven million in Israel, it's likely that over two million Jews currently practice yoga or will in the near future. Additionally, many yoga teachers and trainers are Jewish.

No central organization tracks the number of yoga practitioners globally. However, over 300 million individuals are estimated to engage in yoga, including those who incorporate it into their spiritual or religious beliefs, those who practice for its physical and mental health benefits, or both.

Jewish Confusion

Many yoga schools operate without following a standard definition of yoga or established qualifications for yoga teachers. As a result, individuals can label their practices however they choose, including kosher. At times, classes are held in synagogues, temples, and Jewish community centers. Permitting yoga classes in these locations conveys the message that yoga is acceptable for Jews.

Perspectives on Yoga and Jewish Spirituality

Some authors explore the relationship between yoga and Jewish spirituality. They give their perspectives on the compatibility of yoga with Judaism based on their personal experiences and how they have integrated yoga into their Jewish lives. Some emphasize what they believe are similarities between yoga and Jewish spirituality and how the two complement each other in deepening one's G-dly connection. Others tackle some of the more controversial issues surrounding the integration of yoga into Jewish practice and offer their perspectives. A lack of standardization prevents a clear understanding of what any given class might teach.

The False Pretext of Intention (*Kavanah*)

While some authors acknowledge that yoga is filled with idolatrous practices, they argue that intention (*Kavanah*) is the only or the most significant factor in determining whether participation is halachically problematic. They believe that if one does not recognize the idols in a yoga studio, the spiritual components do not matter. They consider yoga to be an exercise rather than a religious practice.

In a 2010 article for Tablet magazine, Taffy Brodesser-Akner writes that intention is a complex topic in Judaism.

"Intuitively, it would seem that a religion demanding absolute morality would be concerned with intention. But, actually, that's not really the case. If you eat bread on Passover, even accidentally, you have sinned. If you give to charity but grudgingly, the charity still counts for the good. On Yom Kippur, we repent for sins we didn't even know we did. And then there are Hannah's sons—seven Jews who chose to die rather than bow to Antiochus, the Greek ruler who tried to forcibly convert Jews in 167 BCE. Bowing but not meaning it wasn't an option. Judaism is concerned not just with your actions but also very much with how your actions appear to others. Bowing is the physical manifestation of idolatry, whatever your intention. "Do not make idols or set up an image or a sacred stone for yourselves," says Leviticus 26:1, "and do not place a carved stone in your land to bow down before it."[2]

Others acknowledge yoga's Hindu roots and worship of Hindu deities but consider yoga a spiritual practice, not a religion. For them, engaging in Hindu spiritual practices does not mean that they are worshiping Hindu gods.

People more sensitive to these issues may seek out yoga studios that don't have statues, incense, and chanting of

Hindu mantras to warm up, but this doesn't make the practice kosher.

No Such Thing as Kosher Yoga

Yoga originated in India and has been practiced for thousands of years. Its teachings and techniques are rooted in Hindu scriptures, including the Vedas and Upanishads. For example, the primary Hindu scripture, the Bhagavad Gita, states, "Yoga is the journey of the self, through the self, to the self."

Idolatry is one of the three forbidden biblical sins for which, under certain circumstances, a Jew may be required to sacrifice their life rather than commit. Over 50 Torah commandments forbid idol worship or showing any deference to false deities, and eliminating idolatry is a positive commandment.

The Torah also includes examples of how some pagan idols are worshipped. Suppose a Jew performs an action that resembles how a particular idol is worshipped. In that case, he is liable, even if he explicitly states that he does not regard the idol as a deity, even if he intends to demean or degrade it, and even if it is done accidentally.

Yoga's Poses and Postures

There are various types of yoga, each with a specific focus and goal: physical postures (*asanas*), breathing (*pranayama*), meditation, or a combination. However, all forms of yoga ultimately aim for spiritual growth.

Examples of the most well-known yoga poses and the Hindu deities associated with them are as follows:

1. **Sun Salutation (*Surya Namaskar*):** The sun salutation, associated with the god of the sun, is a series of 12 yoga poses performed sequentially. It is often used as a warm-up exercise. According to the *Rigveda*, one of the oldest Hindu texts, *Surya* is "the soul of all that moves and breathes."
2. **Cobra Pose (*Bhujangasana*):** This backbend involves lying on your stomach and lifting your chest off the ground while keeping your arms straight. It is linked to a Hindu deity typically depicted as a many-headed serpent.
3. **Lotus Pose (*Padmasana*):** This pose, linked to two Hindu deities, involves crossing the legs and resting the feet on one's thighs.

The Rebbe's Perspective on Yoga

In a memorandum dated Teveth 5738 (1978), the Rebbe wrote:

> It is well known that certain oriental movements, such as Transcendental Meditation (T. M.), Yoga, Guru, and the like, have attracted many Jewish followers, particularly among the young generation.

In as much as these movements involve certain rites and rituals, they have been rightly regarded by Rabbinic authorities as cults bordering on, and in some respects actual, Avodah Zarah (idolatry). Accordingly, Rabbinic authorities everywhere, and particularly in Eretz Yisroel, ruled that these cults come under all the strictures associated with Avodah Zarah so that also their appurtenances come under strict prohibition (see Appendix A, Letter 1 for the complete document).

In a letter dated May 27, 1979, the Rebbe writes:

Inasmuch as the Torah and mitzvot were given to all the Jews, and to each one individually, for all times and in all places, and "these are our lives and the length of our days," it is clear that every moment of a Jew's life should be consecrated to Torah and mitzvot. Hence it is both surprising and painful to see a Jew spending precious time in search of "greener pastures" elsewhere, even if his intentions are good, for, as above, the important thing is the actual deed.

Needless to say, the above includes Yoga and similar cults even if it is not connected with anything pertaining to avoda zarah—if there is such cult that is completely free from avoda zarah, and in this, only a competent Torah authority who is permeated with halacha is qualified to rule.

I am not seeking opportunities to admonish anyone, but since you mention certain oriental cults, it is my duty to call your attention to the fact that every spare moment that a Jew can use to deepen his knowledge of Torah, he dissipates it on other things is deplorable enough, not to mention cults that in their overwhelming majority are certainly connected with avoda zarah in one way or another, and if there are exceptions, one must make doubly sure through an expert Torah authority, as mentioned above.[3]

Summarizing the Rebbe's position:

1. The overwhelming majority of the oriental-styled practices discussed here relate to Avodah Zarah in one way or another.
2. Determining whether similar practices are entirely free of Avodah Zarah can only be done by a competent Torah authority; thus, the rabbi must be an expert in halacha (Jewish law)—and a *mumcheh* (expert) in this area.
3. Yoga, as we know it, is associated with Avodah Zarah.
4. The life of a Jew is precious and should not be squandered on frivolous activities; rather, it should be devoted to fulfilling Torah and mitzvot.

Rav Yitzchak Ginsburgh, the founder of the Gal Einai Institute in Israel, offers a detailed explanation of why yoga is problematic from a Jewish perspective.

He writes:

> The thoughts we have, the words we choose, and the movements we make profoundly affect and influence our souls. Therefore, as Jews, we have an obligation to ensure that all of these garments (machshava, dibur, and ma'aseh: thought, speech, and action) are kosher in their source.
>
> It is very easy to think that by making alterations to non-kosher things, we have made them kosher. But often, at the very best, we have perhaps removed some of what makes them treif (non-kosher), but there is still a very far and often unbreachable leap between something not being treif and it being kosher. And ultimately, even if it has been accomplished, we must be careful not to refer to it by its treif name and then add the word "kosher."[4]

According to Rav Ginsburgh, stretches and postures aren't the main issues; instead, the names, such as downward dog, cow, camel, and cobra pose, are problematic from a Jewish perspective. Yoga seeks to connect and relate to the animal or deity through thought, speech (in the name), and action. The most concerning poses are those named to honor Hindu sages, like Bharadwaj's Twist or the Half Lord of the Fishes pose, *ardha matsyendrasana*. Moreover, the traditional "warrior" poses are linked to Hindu mythology and stories from the Bhagavad Gita, directly connecting them to idol worship.

Another issue Rav Ginsburgh mentions is that, without a standard definition of yoga, instructors can label the practice however they choose, including Kosher Yoga and Kabbalah Yoga. This can be highly misleading if the teacher is Jewish and not well-versed in halachic issues, or worse, is knowledgeable but chooses to disregard them.

Wrestling with Yoga: Journey of a Jewish Soul

In her informative and deeply personal book, *Wrestling with Yoga: Journey of a Jewish Soul,* Shelly Dembe shares highlights from her years as a yoga teacher and her subsequent religious journey.[5] Dembe illustrates how a typical yoga class concludes: hands clasped in front of the chest in a "prayer position" as the teacher and students say the Sanskrit word "namaste" aloud, followed by bows toward the teacher, who reciprocates.

Observing different translations of *namaste*, Dembe shared the meaning she had understood during her 20-year practice: "I honor the light within you." As her Jewish journey began, she felt uneasy reciting it with her hands in a prayer position and sought to understand the reason behind her discomfort.

Dembe's research revealed that "namaste" is a Hindi greeting combining two Sanskrit words: "nama" (meaning "to bow") and "te" (meaning "you"), which roughly translates to "I bow to you." Even at the beginning of her Jewish journey, she understood that Jews bowed only to G-d, so she informed her students that bowing went against her religion and asked them not to bow to her as their teacher or to each other. From then on, she concluded her classes with "shalom" while bringing her unclasped hands to her heart.

More contraindications came quickly. A Hindu yoga master—a swami—joined her yoga training session to discuss yogic philosophy, and the class included collective chanting. While the vibrations captivated the students, the energy made Dembe uncomfortable. Fortunately, chanting was optional, but her curiosity prompted Dembe to research the English translation of the Sanskrit chant:

> I bow to the lotus feet of the guru who awakens insight into the happiness of pure Being, who is the final refuge, the jungle physician, who eliminates the delusion caused by the poisonous herb of samsara [conditioned existence]. I prostrate before the sage Patanjali who has thousands of radiant, white heads [in his form as the divine serpent,] and who has, as far as his arms, assumed the form of a man holding a conch shell [divine sound], a wheel [discus of light, representing infinite time] and a sword [discrimination].[6]

Memories of chanting in ashrams, yoga studios, and even at home flooded Dembe's mind, prompting her to wonder what else she had proclaimed over the years. The truths she uncovered next were more disturbing and illustrated how easily one can get caught up in a cult-like mentality.

Reflecting on her experiences in various settings, Dembe questioned the extent to which she might have unwittingly proclaimed certain beliefs. While unthinkingly following her yoga instructor, she moved, breathed, and chanted in various ways without understanding their Sanskrit significance, and she felt embarrassed for having participated. Their deep cultural and spiritual significance could not be taken lightly.

Based on her realizations, Dembe's advice for those continuing their yoga practice emphasized the importance of screening what they allow into their bodies while engaging in physical movements, speaking, and thinking. All three elements can fundamentally shape our souls, making it essential to be aware of the environment we create. Essentially, just as we focus on our breath, perform a posture, or chant a mantra, we must also pay close attention to the messages we absorb.[7]

Possible Solutions

As Rabbi Ginsburgh points out, similar or nearly identical poses and stretches in yoga can also be found in other forms of exercise, such as Pilates, barre training, strength training, core workouts, and more. If the objective is to increase flexibility or strength, an exercise program could be crafted to meet those aims using straightforward stretches and movement descriptions while steering clear of Hindu terminology. For instance, nearly every yoga class features Bharadwaj's Twist or the Half Lord of the Fishes pose, which can be easily described as a half-spinal twist.

Rabbi Ginsburgh writes that removing the Buddha from the yoga studio or classroom and refraining from ringing the bells or chimes are insufficient if participants continue to engage in the downward dog pose (which resembles prostration) and inhale and exhale while holding a mountain pose. To assert that one can think about G-d during any of these poses is a contradiction at the most fundamental level. Claiming that "modern yoga" is no longer associated with its original form while still calling it by the same name is akin to saying Jews can celebrate gentile holidays simply because they have become popular in America.[8]

To identify the problem and suggest a solution, Dembe used the standard yoga warm-up sequence (12 connected postures repeated three to five times) known as the Sun Salutation, which begins many yoga classes. The challenge for Jews and all monotheists lies in their origins. Known as *Surya Namaskar* in Sanskrit, this posture (or *asana*) venerates Surya, the "chief solar deity" in Hinduism. *Namaskar*, similar to *namaste*, translates to "bowing to" or "adoring."

The association between the Sun Salutation and its roots in sun god worship has diminished as yoga gained popularity in the Western world during the late 20th century, shifting the practice from a spiritual focus to a physical one. While it's safe to say that most Westerners who practice yoga don't believe they are worshiping or intending to worship the sun or any Hindu deities associated with other poses, Dembe offers practical suggestions. One approach is to modify the warm-up sequence and avoid strict adherence to the set poses that define the Sun Salutation. This allows students to create a practice that serves them rather than merely serving the practice. Not labeling one's warm-up as a "Sun Salutation" or using the Sanskrit name, which more explicitly implies idolatry, can also help.[9]

I have corresponded with a Chassidic yoga teacher who, before becoming religious, lived in an ashram. While she continues to teach, her classes follow Rabbi Ginsburgh's guidelines by refraining from Sanskrit salutations or chanting. She opts not to use the Sanskrit names for poses because of their spiritual significance in Hinduism. Additionally, she avoids referring to the poses by their English names. Rather than saying "downward dog," she tells the student to bend forward with legs and arms straight while lifting the hips.

Additional Points

In 2019, I consulted on the monograph titled "Yoga—Can It Be Kosher?" Machon Shmuel of the Sami Rohr Research Institute published this report.[10] Other halachic issues related to Jewish yoga practice are discussed, including the following.

Chukos Ha-Akum

The Torah prohibits imitating the dress, gatherings, and practices of non-Jews. Yoga, which originated in Hinduism, is linked to Avodah Zarah. Al Tifnu further prohibits associating with idolatrous practices by expressing interest in or learning about them.

Mar'it ayin

Anything that is kosher but looks non-kosher should be avoided to prevent others from getting confused and potentially violating Jewish law. For instance, if a Jew observes other Jews practicing yoga (assuming it's possible to create a completely sanitized version), they might mistakenly think that all yoga is permissible.

Prostration

The prostrations done in yoga practices are halachically prohibited as forms of idolatrous worship or, at the very least, things that resemble idolatry. Mentioning names associated with idolatry is also forbidden.

Incense

The incense used in many yoga practices poses halachic issues due to its associations with idolatry.

Teacher

One must be cautious about choosing one's teacher. While studying a discipline with a non-Jewish instructor does not appear to be explicitly prohibited, it's best to avoid learning from a yoga devotee—whether Jewish or not—who embraces yoga's religious and philosophical dimensions, as this may be forbidden.

Location

Approaching, much less entering, the door of an idolatrous house of worship is prohibited. Consequently, regarding yoga practices, entering a Buddhist temple, a Hindu ashram, or other non-Jewish places of worship is also forbidden. Many yoga studios have statues of the Buddha or Hindu deities. This prohibition likely does not extend to classes held in a gym or similar venues, which don't have idols.

Blurred Lines

Also harmful are misleading articles in Jewish publications that acknowledge yoga's halachic difficulties in passing and then misquote Rabbinic authorities, misrepresenting their views to further their personal agendas. For instance, in a *Jerusalem Post* article, "Yoga and the Jews," Rabbi Ginsburgh's opposition is portrayed as yoga possessing the "dust" of idolatry. The article also cites Rabbi Gutman (Gil) Locks, who asserts that various elements of yoga and its poses are indeed idolatrous. So far, so good—until the author quotes a Jerusalem-based yoga instructor who completely misrepresents the Rebbe's position on yoga.

"While the Lubavitcher Rebbe acknowledged the Hindu roots of yoga," she explained, 'he realized the mental and physical benefits of the practice and gave his followers a *heter* [permission] to practice yogic meditation and movements in more neutral contexts. The mainstream medical community has documented the benefits of mindful movement, thereby normalizing yoga and meditation—and the Rebbe, too, recognized the positive mental and physical benefits that yoga has on those who practice it.'"[11]

In the article "Yoga is Kosher," published in Los Angeles's *The Jewish Journal*, the author conflates the Rebbe's call for medical professionals to develop and promote kosher therapeutic meditation techniques to address stress with the Rebbe giving a heter to practice yoga. This misinterpretation is further compounded by the author's selective use of quotes from the Rebbe's correspondence, which are taken out of context to support the author's argument. These quotes are presented in a way that misleads readers about the Rebbe's actual position on yoga.[12]

The Rebbe's position on yoga as Avodah Zarah (idolatry) is clear, as shown by his confidential memorandum and the letter referenced in this chapter. The author's assertion that the Rebbe granted a heter to practice yoga is a grave disservice to the Rebbe's deep concern that Jews have access to methods for managing stress that are strictly kosher. The Rebbe explicitly stated that he kept his memorandum confidential because it could unintentionally lead someone to infer a heter, which was never his intention.

The authors of both articles neglect to recognize the Rebbe's true intent: to encourage healthcare providers to develop meditation practices that alleviate stress and comply with Jewish law for those who would benefit from them for health and healing.

Alternative Practices for Health and Flexibility

Numerous studies demonstrate the health benefits associated with specific stretches and exercises popularized by yoga, including enhanced flexibility, strength, balance, and cardiovascular health. Additionally, yoga is known to help alleviate stress and anxiety while promoting overall well-being.

When the Rebbe sent his meditation memorandum in the mid-1970s, relatively few Westerners practiced yoga, and its health benefits had yet to be documented. However, given yoga's exponential growth in recent years, it's possible that the Rebbe might welcome the availability of kosher stretches and exercises entirely free from Avodah Zarah, as determined by a Torah authority with expertise in this area.

Rav Ginsburgh writes:

> If a person chooses to exercise and use movements found in yoga, they should be termed by how they work the muscles and joints and affect the body. They should never be called by the terminology of the yoga poses, and the overall movements and exercise should not be referred to as yoga or "kosher yoga."[13]

Instead of modifying yoga, Rav Ginsburgh suggests creating an entirely new exercise system that aligns with Jewish values and spirituality. Over several years, Rabbi Ginsburgh and his students developed a series of movement exercises that provide physical benefits while respecting religious principles.

This innovative approach incorporates stretches and poses inspired by the shapes of Hebrew letters, providing a fully kosher practice. Rabbi Dror Shaul in Dharamshala and Rabbi Zohar David in Rishikesh teach this system in India. The vision is to expand this practice and develop a comprehensive approach integrating body and soul. Designed with universal appeal, this system aims to offer healing and benefits for Jews and non-Jews.[14]

Chapter 15:
Mantra Meditations

This chapter will focus on Transcendental Meditation (TM) as a representative of all Hindu mantra meditations. In a letter to the Rebbe dated March 22, 1978, Dr. Yehuda Landes stated, "I believe that Transcendential (sic) Meditation operated by the Hindu monk, Maharishi Mahesh Yogi, is the most prolific, highly organized, and dangerous of the groups." Although it is experiencing a downward spiral from its peak in the mid-1970s in terms of Jewish exposure, TM remains the best-organized, most well-funded, and most dangerous form of Eastern meditation. Celebrities and business leaders are cultivated as part of their marketing strategy. However, yoga and mindfulness have left it far behind in terms of numbers and reach.

I am an expert in Transcendental Meditation (TM). In 1974, I trained for six months with TM's guru to become a TM teacher, and from 1975 to 1979, I was a senior executive in the national TM organization. More recently, I acted as an expert witness for the plaintiffs in a class action lawsuit stemming from the teaching of TM in the Chicago Public Schools. I am aware of TM's deep Hindu roots and its denial of these origins as part of its marketing strategy.

Transcendental Meditation (TM) is marketed as a simple technique for relaxation and self-improvement, drawing followers from various religious backgrounds. However,

TM's ties to Hinduism and its religious foundations raise significant concerns for Jews.

The Mantra

The mantra (focus word) is central to TM and is mentally repeated during meditation. In his book *Strength in Stillness: The Power of Transcendental Meditation*, Bob Roth, the CEO of the David Lynch Foundation, describes the mantra as a word or sound without meaning.[1] The Foundation promotes TM practices in public schools and veterans' organizations.

TM mantras do have meanings. They are names of Hindu deities, yet this information is deliberately withheld from prospective TM students. In 1955, Maharishi, the featured speaker at a Hindu religious gathering in Kerala, India, acknowledged that TM mantras are not only names of Hindu deities but are also intended to invoke the influence of Hindu gods in the practitioner's life.

> But we do not select the sound at random. We do not select any sound like "mike, flower, table, pen, wail," etc., because such ordinary sounds can do nothing more than merely sharpening the mind . . . For our practice, we select only the suitable mantras of personal gods. Such mantras fetch to us the grace of personal gods.[2]

Puja Initiation Ceremony

Learning TM requires mandatory student participation in a Hindu worship service called a *puja*. During this ceremony, 16 offerings are made to a pantheon of Hindu deities and gurus. The TM teacher chants the puja in Sanskrit, but students do not receive a translation of the ceremony, not even upon request.

Memorizing the puja is a non-negotiable part of becoming a TM teacher, and we were tested until we got it. Additionally, we had to learn the hand movements for the 16 offerings performed during the ceremony, and we were encouraged to evoke different emotions with each offering. The entire process embodies reverence.

In *Strength in Stillness: The Power of Transcendental Meditation*, Roth minimizes the religious significance of the puja:

> Also, during this initial meeting, your teacher will talk about the tradition of great meditation teachers who have safeguarded the knowledge of transcendence for millennia and about the traditional way a TM teacher acknowledges this lineage of teachers today. Prior to the instruction, your teacher will perform a simple thank-you ceremony—an ancient way of expressing gratitude to the teacher. It's a lovely cultural tradition, and not religious in any way... You won't, of course, be asked to participate in it. The

> thank-you includes a few flowers, some fresh fruit, a candle, a stick of incense, and, to represent the tradition of meditation teachers, a picture of Maharishi's teacher, Guru Dev. I have instructed many hundreds of devoutly religious people of all faiths, and when I describe the ceremony, some initially think it could be religious. But when I explain its purpose, they appreciate it.[3]

Contrary to Roth's assertion that Transcendental Meditation (TM) is not religious, one need only examine the Sanskrit translation of the puja. During my teacher training course, we watched videos of Maharishi Mahesh Yogi stating that the puja inserted the influence of Hindu deities into the lives of TM initiates. Furthermore, Maharishi was believed to assert that the puja created a mystical connection with Guru Dev, his long-deceased teacher, ultimately establishing Maharishi as the true teacher or guru. Although this was not taught in my teacher training program, course leaders confirmed it.

During my training course, we learned to subtly encourage students to kneel before Guru Dev's photo. At the end of the ceremony, I made a sweeping gesture, inviting my students to join me in kneeling. While it wasn't required, most of my TM students chose to kneel.

As noted in the Roth quote, "You won't, of course, be asked to participate in it." Roth suggests that TM students are merely passive witnesses to the puja. However, students must bring flowers, a white cloth, and two pieces of fruit to the ceremony, all of which are used in the offerings during the ritual. In Hinduism, the use of these items as offerings to the deities worshipped in the puja is referred to as Dakshina. Dakshina alters the student's status, even if unwittingly, to that of a full-fledged participant.

The Establishment Clause

The religious nature of Transcendental Meditation (TM) has been legally recognized. In Malnak v. Yogi, decided in 1977, a federal court ruled that TM qualifies as a religious practice and violates the Establishment Clause of the First Amendment of the U.S. Constitution when taught in public schools. The court determined that the puja and TM's philosophical framework, the Science of Creative Intelligence, are Hindu religious practices. An appeal made by the TM organization to a higher court was unsuccessful.[4]

The Rebbe was aware of the case and attached a copy of the court's decision to his Confidential Memorandum.

The First Amendment's Establishment Clause was recently at the center of a significant legal case. The Chicago Public Schools and the David Lynch Foundation reached a $2.6 million settlement in a class action lawsuit. This lawsuit was filed on behalf of 710 students who received Transcendental Meditation instruction at their schools, arguing that such instruction infringed upon their First Amendment rights. As mentioned above, I acted as an expert witness for the plaintiff. (U. S. DISTRICT COURT, NORTHERN DISTRICT OF ILL. EASTERN DIV. **CASE NO. 23 C 218**)

Fraudulent Promises of Superpowers

The TM Sidhi program was introduced in 1977, with costs averaging $15,000 in 2024 dollars. Maharishi promoted the program by promising participants the development of superpowers, such as levitation (hovering in mid-air), super vision and hearing, invisibility, and the strength of an elephant. During 1977–78, hundreds of advertisements appeared in campus publications and mainstream newspapers across the U.S. and Canada. The images in these newspaper ads were altered to create the illusion of levitation.

There were also press conferences where TM teachers claimed they could levitate but were too modest to provide a demonstration. In 1977, Maharishi, appearing on the then-popular Merv Griffin television show, asserted that Sidhas (those who had learned the Siddha formulas) would be able to fly through the sky. This was a completely fraudulent statement.

Landes brought TM's claim of flying to the Rebbe's attention. In a meeting on May 1, 1980, with Dr. Chaim Rosen and Dr. Seymour Applebaum, the discussion included a claim made by "a certain Lubavitcher that the Rebbe had told him privately that certain forms of meditation could enable people to fly, practice mind control, and communicate telepathically." Everyone at the meeting expressed concern.

Dr. Landes sent a mailgram to the Rebbe requesting clarification. Shortly afterward, the Rebbe replied with a telegram:

> Dr. Landes
>
> [6 May, 1980 (20 Iyar, 5740)]
>
> In reply to your mailgram 5-1-80 [which was] just received, though self-evident from our personal discussions and correspondence, I must emphasize again, that my views and guidelines [in] reference [to] T.M. Meditation have not and could not have been changed, since they are based on [the] Shulchan Aruch.
>
> As for the suggestion you mention in your telegram about "teaching people to fly," it is the first I hear about it, nor do I know details of it. But, needless to say, if it implies physical flying, and hence delusional, it is not only contrary to Torah—as [is] any deception—but also inadvisable as a therapeutic method. Since, eventually, the patient will realize the deception and it is bound to result in a severe reaction.
>
> With blessing,

The Rebbe maintained his position on his fundamental concerns regarding Avodah Zarah in relation to TM.

However, this did not lessen his appreciation for the therapeutic benefits of meditation. As discussed in earlier chapters, rather than a sweeping condemnation, the Rebbe advocated for developing "kosher meditation." He believed that the idolatrous elements present in TM were irrelevant to the benefits achievable through its core technique. Dr. Herbert Benson had already demonstrated this in his book, The Relaxation Response. By promoting this approach, the Rebbe aimed to provide Jews with an effective means of managing stress through meditation while avoiding spiritual pitfalls.

In summary, Jews who engage in TM or other Eastern mantra meditations risk unknowingly participating in the worship of foreign gods and being exposed to a religious philosophy that contradicts Judaism's most fundamental principles. This carries several broader implications.

- First, the potential for spiritual confusion arises because Judaism is a monotheistic religion with a clear set of beliefs and practices. By invoking multiple deities and emphasizing a guru-disciple relationship, TM introduces foreign spiritual concepts that can blur a Jew's religious focus. For a Jew who is not well-established in Jewish tradition, this confusion can dilute an individual's practice and beliefs, creating inner spiritual conflict.

- Second, TM directly violates the Jewish prohibition against idolatry. Mantras that invoke Hindu deities and participating in the puja ceremony constitute acts of Avodah Zarah.

- Third, the risk of syncretism—the blending of different religious practices—poses a significant concern when Jews engage in non-Jewish spiritual activities. Promising spiritual enlightenment through a technique rooted in Hinduism, Transcendental Meditation (TM) may lead Jews to incorporate Hindu concepts and practices into their lives. The potential outcome is a distortion of Jewish observance and a threat to the integrity of the Jewish faith.

TM serves as a warning about the dangers of religious or spiritual deception. Thorough due diligence is paramount before adopting any spiritual practice.

In a world of interfaith exploration and spiritual seeking, Jews must recognize the potential pitfalls. While pursuing spirituality and self-improvement is praiseworthy, these undertakings should be approached with care and discernment. For Jews, this means staying grounded in the principles of Judaism and avoiding practices contradicting Jewish law and beliefs. The story of TM illustrates how prioritizing market share over honesty can lead to the deliberate concealment of foreign religious practices, posing significant dangers to unsuspecting consumers who are simply searching for a way to cope with stress.

Chapter 16: Mindfulness and Mindfulness-Based Stress Release

Mindfulness is a Buddhist practice, and the contrast between Judaism and Buddhism is striking. Buddhism's ultimate goal is personal enlightenment. In Buddhism, there is no concept of a personal G-d as understood in Judaism. Buddhist teachings emphasize that the path to enlightenment is one individuals must walk for themselves without reliance on divine intervention, as there is no divinity.

While Buddhism does not have a concept of a personal G-d in the monotheistic sense, it embraces a complex and multifaceted belief in a spiritual universe and the various beings that inhabit it. Many aspects of Buddhism involve practices that could be considered idolatrous or bear a close resemblance to them. For example, Buddhist temples feature statues of the Buddha and altars where various offerings are made.

Mindfulness-Based Stress Reduction

Imagine a practice grounded in Buddhist beliefs and ultimate goals but reframed as a secular, science-based technique for reducing stress and enhancing focus. Welcome to the world of Mindfulness-Based Stress Reduction, or MBSR. With claims of empirically validated benefits, MBSR has become very successful in American schools and corporations. Yet, beneath the surface of secular self-help lies a more complex reality. Mindfulness advocates have achieved mainstream acceptance through strategic ambiguity, selective framing, and minimizing their Buddhist roots. This reflects a deception with far-reaching consequences.

At the core of the mindfulness deception lies a bait-and-switch tactic. It is marketed as a secular practice that promises stress relief and cognitive enhancement based on scientific research. However, looking deeper, a more religiously charged agenda comes to light. Prominent mindfulness advocates portray mindfulness as a means of mainstreaming Buddhist teachings. Depending on the audience, they engage in "code-switching," adjusting their message to emphasize science to secular groups while presenting mindfulness as a covert way to convey Buddhism to Buddhist-friendly audiences.

As Candy Gunther Brown, a professor of religious studies at Indiana University, writes,

> When speaking to Buddhist audiences, promoters describe their tactics as "skillful means," "stealth Buddhism," a "Trojan horse," or a "script." These spokespersons exhibit what linguists term "code switching" and sociologists call "frontstage/backstage" behavior—moving between vocabularies of multiple cultures to achieve complex goals.

> As psychologist Daniel Goleman boasts of his efforts, "The Dharma is so disguised that it could never be proven in court."[1]

The Goleman quote is especially troubling because it suggests that Goleman integrated Buddhist principles into his work in psychology and emotional intelligence, yet did so subtly enough that it wouldn't be obvious to readers.

It's a shell game with the religious ball hidden beneath a secular cup. However, the deception runs even deeper. Promoters deny participants proper informed consent by obscuring the practice's religious roots and societal objectives. Under the guise of secular self-help, this approach ultimately reveals itself as pure paternalism—using stress reduction to justify strategic ambiguity and calculated dishonesty.

This strategic ambiguity allows mindfulness to appear nonreligious while still evoking the gravitas of its Buddhist heritage for those aware of its roots. For example, Jon Kabat-Zinn's widely accepted definition of mindfulness as "paying attention in a particular way: on purpose, in the present moment, and nonjudgmentally" removes overt Buddhist connotations while still implying a depth and richness derived from its Buddhist origins context.[2]

Mindfulness advocates have used scientific research and terminology to build credibility and secular legitimacy. They have positioned mindfulness as an evidence-based practice aligned with contemporary secular values by highlighting neuroimaging studies, clinical trials, and measurable outcomes such as stress reduction and improved focus. This approach has proven effective, resulting in increased acceptance of mindfulness in schools and healthcare settings and securing funding from corporations and foundations.

Promoters have often minimized or denied the religious aspects of mindfulness to address potential objections. This has involved steering clear of explicit Buddhist terminology, renouncing religious intentions, and likening mindfulness to universally accepted activities like sports or music to appear secular by association. Such comparisons obscure mindfulness's Buddhist roots and imply a harmlessness and universality that do not reflect the practice's religious and spiritual depth and implications.

Jon Kabat-Zinn's statements exemplify this code-switching. He alternately describes his Mindfulness-Based Stress Reduction (MBSR) program as either a secular therapeutic approach or a means of bringing Buddha-dharma (the teachings, principles, and practices of Buddhism) into the mainstream. This strategic ambiguity allows promoters to simultaneously gain acceptance in secular circles while nurturing a deeper religious and philosophical dimension for those already inclined.

By stripping away what Kabat-Zinn refers to as "unnecessary historical and cultural baggage," MBSR preserves the essential aspects that are co-extensive, if not identical, with the teachings of Buddhism. As he stated in another interview, "What we're really trying to do is to create an American Dharma, an American Zen."[3]

The training process for MBSR instructors further highlights the religiosity of mindfulness. Although the public representation of MBSR emphasizes secular science, the training journey for instructors entails immersion in Buddhist teachings and practices. Prospective instructors must first complete an eight-week MBSR course as participants. They then engage in an intensive teacher training program, which includes extended Buddhist or other meditation retreats and the study of Buddhist texts.

Westerners have reduced mindfulness to a self-help tool for personal success and happiness. In Buddhist practice, meditation is a component of a broader spiritual framework aimed at transcending the ego. In a fundamental disconnect, Western culture has redefined mindfulness to reinforce the ego and assist people in becoming more competitive within a consumer-driven society.

The Role of Thought in Judaism Contrasted with MBSR

MBSR and Judaism approach the meaning and importance of thought in fundamentally different ways.

In MBSR, thoughts are seen as fleeting, transitory mental experiences that arise and dissipate in the present moment. They are not considered inherently good or bad, nor problematic or harmful; instead, they represent a continually changing flow of experience. They hold no intrinsic value.

Judaism provides a different perspective. Thought and intellectual inquiry are highly valued in Jewish tradition. The Talmud, a central text in Judaism, is rich with intricate debates and legal reasoning, showcasing a deep appreciation for the power of the human mind.

However, Judaism also acknowledges the potential dangers of thought, especially when it leads to sinful or destructive behavior. The Talmud cautions against sinful thoughts and desires, suggesting that merely thinking something negative can be sinful, sometimes even more so than the actual deed.

Another critical difference between MBSR and Judaism is their understanding of the self and its relationship to thought. MBSR sees the self as impermanent and devoid of an inherent, unchanging essence. This perspective promotes a sense of detachment and non-identification with thoughts. Practitioners are encouraged to observe their thoughts without judgment or attachment, rather than engaging with them.

Judaism acknowledges the impermanence of the physical self while affirming the existence of a soul that continues beyond the body. Thoughts are considered capable of influencing the soul either positively or negatively. Positive thoughts and intentions can promote spiritual growth and closeness to G-d, whereas negative thoughts may result in the opposite.

Given these differing perspectives, MBSR and Judaism promote different approaches to engaging with thoughts. MBSR encourages practitioners to observe thoughts as they arise in the present moment without judgment or reaction. The goal is not to change or control thoughts but to cultivate a sense of non-identification or detachment from them. Through this process, MBSR suggests that individuals can achieve greater peace and well-being by freeing themselves from their thoughts.

Judaism values self-awareness and emphasizes thoughtful reflection to achieve positive and ethical outcomes. This includes studying the Torah and other Jewish texts, which guide thinking and acting in a morally upright manner. Judaism promotes prayer and meditation, which direct the mind toward feelings of gratitude, awe, and a connection to G-d. The goal is to nurture positive thoughts and intentions that encourage personal and spiritual growth.

While mindfulness research highlights numerous health benefits, it shares the same shortcomings as other meditation research discussed in Chapter 12. Even if mindfulness proves to be an effective tool for managing emotionally charged thoughts, it should not be embraced as a lifestyle or used to disconnect from one's thoughts.

Jewish Mindfulness—Kavanah

Kavanah, a central concept in Jewish prayer and spiritual practice, is often translated as "intention" or "direction of the heart." Yet, its meaning runs much deeper. At its core, kavanah involves cultivating focused attention and sincerity in one's religious practices, particularly in prayer and the performance of mitzvot (commandments). The practice of kavanah extends beyond the religious realm, encouraging us to approach all aspects of life with greater intention and presence. It invites us to engage with the world using our whole selves and to uncover deeper meaning and purpose in our daily experiences.

In our distracted, multitasking-oriented culture, kavanah provides a way to remain anchored in the present moment instead of getting lost in future worries or past regrets. Through this practice, we cultivate a deeper awareness of our thoughts, feelings, and actions, discovering more profound meaning in our daily experiences.

The practice of kavanah is a journey, not a destination. Unlike MBSR, thought in Judaism is not something to observe while waiting for feelings or associations to fade. Judaism is not a spectator sport. Kavanah empowers us to engage fully in our lives rather than merely witness them.

Chapter 17: The Power That Made the Body Heals the Body

It Happens No Other Way

Throughout this book, we explored Rabbi Menachem Schneerson's transformative teachings, uncovering powerful tools for health, healing, and well-being. Meditation, positivity, and the power of belief offer a toolkit for managing stress and nurturing resilience in today's high-stress world.

Nearly five decades ago, the Rebbe called for a "kosher" therapeutic meditation to combat the debilitating effects of stress. This was not intended to be a Jewish meditation. There were two primary purposes. The first was to provide an effective way to alleviate stress, and the second was to offer an alternative for Jews drawn to gurus and Eastern spiritual paths, many of whom ultimately became involved in cults. The initial emphasis on stress reduction promoted by these gurus often served as a gateway to deeper involvement.

The Rebbe sought to develop a meditation that could compete with Transcendental Meditation, which had, at the time, attracted tens of thousands of Jews. He focused on creating a kosher meditation rather than a new Jewish one. Here, kosher refers to a meditation free from undesirable elements or concepts regarded as idolatrous, concentrating solely on the essential healing aspect—the technique itself.

Today, as stress reaches epidemic levels, his vision is more relevant than ever. Fifty years ago, the kosher meditation technique he sought seemed to elude him. I believe the meditation practice presented in this book is what he was searching for. It is simple to learn and effective against stress, and the gentle interplay between a focus word and thought mirrors the method I learned while training as a teacher of Transcendental Meditation. However, there are no initiation ceremonies, Hindu mantras, or engagement with Eastern spiritual practices or philosophy; in other words, there is no trace of Avodah Zarah. Regular practice can unlock deep relaxation, therapeutic benefits, and a sense of calm that remains with you throughout your day and life.

But meditation is only the beginning. The Rebbe's teachings highlight the significance of positivity, the strength of belief, and reframing challenges as opportunities for growth. By altering your mindset, you can actively engage in your wellness journey, building resilience and reducing the impact of stress and anxiety in your life.

As we reduce the stress that drains our energy and become more at ease, we can participate more fully in our daily lives and boost our productivity. With increased energy, we gain more resources to build stronger, healthier families and communities.

The self-help methods presented in this book are supported by decades of research demonstrating that regular practice reduces stress, the leading cause of illness in the world today. However, their potential can only be realized when you incorporate them into your daily routine. The journey to health and healing is a lifelong path—let the Rebbe's teachings be your guide.

A Message to Healthcare Providers

The Rebbe's call to action is more relevant now than ever. It's time to raise awareness about the healing power of mind–body medicine and integrate it into your practices. There's no need to wait for more research to trickle down through medical journals. Ample scientific evidence already exists showing that these methods can play an essential role in health and well-being.

There is an epidemic of stress-related illnesses affecting all your patients; too many are being crippled by it. You, more than anyone, understand that prescription drugs only address symptoms and often lead to a cascade of side effects that require even more medications.

Dr. Benson used a three-legged stool as a metaphor. Medication served as one leg, surgery as the second, and mind-body tools as the third. All three are essential. However, the first two concentrate on illness; this book's mind-body tools empower your patients to heal, build resilience, and enjoy an improved quality of life. You are uniquely positioned to carry forward the Rebbe's message, written nearly 50 years ago:

> Appropriate action be undertaken to enlist the cooperation of a group of doctors specializing in neurology and psychiatry who

would research the said methods with a view to perfecting them and adopting them in their practice on a wider scale.

All due publicity be given about the availability of such methods from practicing doctors.

This should be done most expeditiously, without waiting for this vital information to be disseminated through medical journals, where research and findings usually take a long time before they come to the attention of practicing physicians. This would all the sooner counteract the untold harm done to so many Jews who are attracted daily to the said cults, as mentioned in the opening paragraph.

In conclusion: This memo is intended for all Rabbis, doctors, and laypeople who are in a position to advance the cause espoused herein, the importance of which needs no further elaboration.

Needless to say, even if one feels doubtful whether he can advance this cause, or whether the expectation warrants the effort — the vital importance and urgency of saving so many souls from Avodah Zarah, not only warrants but dictates every possible effort, even if there be a doubt about achieving success; certainly when there is every reason to believe that much, indeed, can be achieved, with G-d's help and Zechus Harabbim [the merit of the many].

Appendix A: Letters from the Rebbe on Meditation

Much of the Rebbe's meditation correspondence comprises an exchange of letters between the Rebbe and Dr. Yehuda Landes, a psychologist from Palo Alto, California. I know of eight letters from the Rebbe to Dr. Landes, most of which are single-spaced and two to three pages long, with many containing the Rebbe's handwritten notes in the margin.

Dr. Landes' letters to the Rebbe included an overview of Eastern meditation practices, popular psychological treatment modalities, and detailed plans for a Jewish meditation institute. While initially encouraging, the Rebbe ultimately shifted direction from the healing center due to the prohibitive costs relative to its perceived impact and the anticipated lengthy start-up time. These letters are referenced in an article by Dr. Landes's son, Rabbi Yehoshua Landes, titled "The Inside Story of the Founding of Jewish Meditation." They are not included here.

This appendix contains the confidential memorandum and its cover letter that the Rebbe sent to mental health professionals. Following this, there is a curated selection of letters in which the Rebbe discusses Zen meditation, yoga, the importance of discouraging Jewish involvement in cults, meditation-related questions, the use of LSD for mystical insight, and guidance on finding one's life path. Unless stated otherwise, all letters are reproduced from photocopies of the original documents.

The Rebbe Responsa team wrote the introduction and meticulously prepared all notes and explanations for the entire correspondence. Below are their notes. This correspondence was first released as a wedding memento (Pape, 18 Adar, 5784). The complete correspondence is accessible at RebbeResponsa.com.

We sincerely thank RebbeResponsa.com for granting permission to reprint this correspondence.

List of Correspondence

Letter 1: Confidential Memorandum dated Teveth 5738 (December 1977)

Letter 2: Cover Letter to Confidential Memorandum dated 16th of Adar 1, 5738 (February 23, 1979) addressed to Dr. Yehuda Landes

Letter 3: Additional letter and telegram dated 19 Tammuz 5739, castigating claims of physical flying by Transcendental Meditation guru (July 14, 1979)

Letter 4: The Rebbe's letter to Chaim Rosen, Ph.D., dated 24th of Teves, 5742 (January 19, 1982)

Additional letters on meditation, yoga, cults, and related topics:

Letter 5: Jewish meditation and Zen, dated 9 Kislev

Letter 6: Seeking yoga and other cults, dated Rosh Chodesh Sivan, 5739

Letter 7: Saving Jews from cults, excerpt from a letter dated 9th of Tammuz, 5740

Letter 8: Nothing is being done to stop cults even after a public outcry, excerpt from a letter dated 11th of Tishrei, 5741

Letter 9: Can I find my own way in life? dated 28 Av, 5740

Letter 10: Meditation as therapy, two letters dated 14 Tammuz, 5738, and 6 Adar, 5739, respectively

Letter 11: Questions on meditation, dated 6 Elul 5731

Letter 12: Using LSD to attain mystical inspiration, dated 20 Marcheshvan, 5725

Transcription of the 13 Tammuz, 5739 (July 8, 1979) talk on kosher meditation

Letter 1[1]

The following[25] is the text of the original memorandum penned by the Rebbe:

CONFIDENTIAL[2] MEMORANDUM

By the Grace of G-d

Teveth, 5738

---

[1] A note on the letters: The member of the Rebbe's secretariat entrusted with transcribing the English letters often used the British spelling, for he spent time and studied in the U.K. before arriving in America. To stay as true as possible to the original we have not amended this spelling and they are scattered throughout (e.g. practised instead of practiced).

The letters published, unless otherwise noted, are sourced in photocopies of the original letters sent.

[2] See above footnote 10.

It is well known that certain oriental movements, such as Transcendental Meditation (T. M.),[3] Yoga, Guru, and the like, have attracted many Jewish followers, particularly among the young generation.[4]

Inasmuch as these movements involve certain rites and rituals, they have been rightly regarded by Rabbinic authorities as cults bordering on and in some respects actual, Avodah Zarah (idolatry). Accordingly, Rabbinic authorities everywhere, and particularly in Eretz Yisroel, ruled that these cults come under all the strictures associated with Avodah Zarah, so that also their appurtenances (אביזרייהו) come under strict prohibition.[5]

Moreover, the United States Federal Court also ruled recently that such movements, by virtue of embracing certain rites and rituals, must be classified as cultic and

---

[3] Transcendental Meditation (TM) is a form of silent meditation (it was so named to separate it from Hinduism or any other religious practice (see further in this memorandum)). The TM technique involves the silent repetition of a mantra or sound, and is practiced for 15–20 minutes twice per day while sitting with the eyes closed.

The Rebbe noted that they gave it a "refined" name: Transcendental, meaning transcending intelligence and logic, above any limitations (*Sichos Kodesh,* op. cit., p. 315).

[4] Though Jews in America account for a small fraction of the general population (two-three percent), the number of Jews involved was estimated at somewhere between twenty and fifty percent (see estimates and sources quoted in Ophir, 111).

[5] See sources quoted above fn. 8.

religious movements. (Cf. Malnak v. Maharishi Mahesh Yogi, U.S.D.C. of N.J. 76-341, esp. pp. 36-50, 78).[6]

On the other hand, certain aspects of the said movements, which are entirely irrelevant to religious worship or practices, have a therapeutic value, particularly in the area of relieving mental stress.

It follows that if these therapeutic methods – insofar as they are utterly devoid of any ritual implications – would be adopted by doctors specializing in the field of mental illness, it would have a two-pronged salutary effect: Firstly, in view of the fact that these methods are therapeutically effective, while there are, regretfully, many who could benefit from such treatment, this is a matter of healing of the highest order, since it has to do with mental illness. It would, therefore, be very wrong to deny such treatment, to those who need it, when it could be given by a practicing doctor.

Secondly, and this too is not less important, since there are many Jewish sufferers who continue to avail themselves of these methods through the said cults despite the Rabbinic prohibition, it can be assumed with certainty that many of them, if not all, who are drawn to these cults by the promise

---

[6] The Rebbe included an excerpt of these court documents and sent them together with the memorandum. Page 78 reads as follows:
Although defendants have submitted well over 1500 pages of briefs, affidavits, and deposition testimony in opposing plaintiffs' motion for summary judgment, defendants have failed to raise the slightest doubt as to the facts or as to the religious nature of the teachings of the Science of Creative Intelligence and the puja. The teaching of the SCI/TM course in New Jersey public high schools violates the establishment clause of the First Amendment, and its teaching must be enjoined.

of mental relief, would prefer to receive the same treatment from the medical profession – if they had a choice of getting it the kosher way.[7] It would thus be possible to save many Jews from getting involved with the said cults.

It is also known, though not widely, that there are individual doctors who practise the same or similar methods as T.M. and the like.

However, it seems that these methods occupy a secondary or subordinate role in their procedures. More importantly, there is almost a complete lack of publicity regarding the application of these methods by doctors, and since the main practice of these doctors is linked with the conventional neurological and psychiatric approach, it is generally assumed that whatever success they achieve is not connected with results obtained from methods relating to T. M. and the like; results which the cults acclaim with such fanfare.

In light of the above, it is suggested and strongly urged that:

(1) Appropriate action be undertaken to enlist the cooperation of a group of doctors specializing in neurology and psychiatry who would research the said methods with a view to perfecting them and adopting them in their practice on a wider scale.

---

[7] The Rebbe later noted that these days the concept of a deliberate renegade does not exist (see sources cited in *Igros Kodesh*, vol. 2, letter 267, part 3). Rather Jews, nowadays, turn away from Judaism out of convenience. It is thus certain that if there is an equally convenient and appealing kosher way Jews will turn to there first (*Sichos Kodesh*, op. cit., p. 320).

(2) All due publicity be given about the ability of such methods from practicing doctors.

(3) This should be done most expeditiously, without waiting for this vital information to be disseminated through medical journals, where research and findings usually take a long time before they come to the attention of practising physicians. This would all the sooner counteract the untold harm done to so many Jews who are attracted daily to the said cults, as mentioned in the opening paragraph.

In conclusion: This Memo is intended for all Rabbis, doctors, and laymen who are in a position to advance the cause espoused herein, the importance of which needs no further elaboration.

Needless to say, even if one feels doubtful whether he can advance this cause, or whether the expectation warrants the effort – the vital importance and urgency of saving so many souls from Avodah Zarah, not only warrants but dictates every possible effort, even if there be a doubt or double doubt about achieving success;[8]

---

[8] See also *Sichos Kodesh*, op. cit., p. 321.

Letter 2

A few weeks after the memorandum was prepared, the Rebbe sent it to Dr. Yehudah Landes, together with the following cover letter:

By the Grace of G-d[33]

16th of Adar I, 5738

Brooklyn, N.Y.

Greeting and Blessing:

It is some time since I heard from you,[34] and I trust that all is well. It is surely unnecessary to add that insofar as a Jew is concerned "all is well" includes, above all, advancement in Torah and Mitzvoth in the everyday life.

The purpose of this letter is to send you the enclosed memorandum which is self explanatory.

The reason it has been written as a separate piece, without signature, and to some extent confidentially, is that the subject matter is of a sensitive nature and the Memo could be used to encourage that which it seeks to discourage and preclude, namely, involvement in Eastern cults. For it may be argued by many who are already involved in the therapy discussed in the Memo, or are tempted to become involved, that until such time as the medical profession will openly adopt the same methods of treatment and provide an alternative, they are justified in seeking this therapy elsewhere, especially if they take care to avoid active participation in the idolatrous rites and ceremonies that go with it. In support of this contention they could cite this Memo which (1) confirms the therapeutic value of a part of the said methods, and (2) indicates also that the idolatrous elements in the said cults are not germane, indeed non-essential, to the therapy itself.

For this reason I am asking you - as all others whom I intend to approach in this matter - to use your discretion in connection with the enclosed Memo, as to its source and its utilization, etc.

I must however point out with all due emphasis that in my opinion the problem has reached such proportions that time is extremely important. Every minute that could be saved in speeding the implementation of the program suggested in the Memo could be a matter of spiritual Pikuach-nefesh for many actual and potential victims of the said cults.

You are one of a select few whom I am approaching in this matter, knowing of your position of influence and connections with this section of the medical profession, which could be used to great advantage and effect in promoting the cause espoused in the Memo - which, I feel certain, will meet with your approval. And the Zechus Horabim will help further.[35]

Needless to say, on my part I will do all I can to mobilize all possible cooperation in behalf of this cause which, I strongly believe, should be pursued with the utmost vigor, without fear of duplication, or overdoing it.

Your comments on all above will be most welcome.

With esteem and blessing,

---

33. This letter is mostly a loose translation of the cover letter sent to Rabbi Dr.Twersky published in Igros Kodesh, vol. 33, letter 12,341 (pp. 119-120).

This letter, as the memorandum, was marked as confidential for the reasons spelled out in this letter. The reasons why we nevertheless published this correspondence are outlined above (note 7).

34. The previous correspondence that we have is a letter of the Rebbe to Dr. Landes is dated Rosh Chodesh Adar II, 5736.

35 The recipient's son reported that until receiving this letter, his father, a psychologist with a conservative outlook, gave little or any credence to alternative forms of therapy, including meditation (Landes, 174).

Letter 3

On May 1, 1980 (15 Iyar 5740), Dr. Rosen, Dr. Landes, and Dr. Applebaum were meeting regarding meditation. One of the things that came up were a claim by a certain Lubavitcher that the Rebbe had told him in private that certain forms of meditation could allow people to fly, to practice mind control and telepathy. Everyone at the meeting was concerned. That day Dr. Landes sent a telegram to the Rebbe asking for clarification. Shortly afterward the Rebbe responded with a telegram:[9]

Dr. [Landes][10]

[6 May, 1980 (20 Iyar, 5740)]

In reply to your mailgram 5-1-80 [which was] just received, though self- evident from our personal discussions and correspondence, I must emphasize again, that my views and guidelines [in] reference [to] T.M. Meditation have not and could not have been changed, since they are based on [the] Shulchan Aruch.

---

[9] Landes, 182.

[10] This telegram is published in *Letters From the Rebbe*, Vol. 6, p. 156, and partially in Landes, 183. We have added additional connecting word [in brackets] and punctuation for easier reading.

As for the suggestion you mention in your telegram about "teaching people to fly," it is the first I hear about it, nor do I know details of it. But, needless to say, if it implies physical flying, and hence delusional, it is not only contrary to Torah — as [is] any deception — but also inadvisable as a therapeutic method. Since, eventually, the patient will realize the deception and it is bound to result in a severe reaction.

With blessing,

Menachem Schneerson

Ultimately, after Dr. Landes and Dr. Rosen conducted several JM workshops in the States, the people involved in Jewish Meditation parted ways. Dr. Rosen made a JM Center in Safed (see letter to him dated 24 Teves, 5742) and Dr. Landes continued in the states, mainly in California, until he retired due to his health in the 1990s.[11]

---

[11] Landes, 182.

Letter 4

By the Grace of G-d

24th of Teves, 5742

Brooklyn. N. Y.

Dr. Chaim Rosen, Ph.D.

Greeting and Blessing:

After the long interval, I was especially pleased to receive your letter of Jan. 8th. May G-d, whose benevolent Providence extends to each and everyone, lead you in the way of the fullest utilization of your abilities to help others, and help yourself, **in strictest accord** with the Torah, **Toras Chaim**. This is also the way of Hatzlocho in the fulfillment of your heart's desires for good.

I have underscored the words "in strict accord," because in the field of Jewish Meditation one cannot overemphasize the great caution that is required to steer clear from even the slightest admixture of Avoda Zara, or even the suspicion of A. Z. I bring this up here because I have received complaints about some practitioners of Jewish Meditation, including also the Jewish Meditation Center of Safed, that, in the view of the complainant, some aspects of the practices are not in accord with the Shulchan Aruch. I do not know the writer personally, but since we are dealing with a highly sensitive and serious area, I cannot ignore such reports. Moreover, it appears that the complaints are basically connected with the fact that those who practice Jewish Meditation are persons who, inevitably, are not the experts on Halacha, particularly on the intricacies of Avoda Zara. Of course, however well meaning a Jew is, the fact that one is an M.D. or Ph. D. clearly indicates that he had devoted considerable time to obtain these degrees, and, to that extent, he has not been able to consecrate all his time and attention to Torah and Halacha. I use the term "consecrate" advisedly, for this is what proper Torah-study demands.

For this reason, it has been my advice to those Ph.D.'s and M.D.'s who wish to enter the field of Jewish Meditation, that even if they also have Rabbinical Ordination (**Smichah**), they should seek the advice and guidance of a competent and experienced Rav, who is an expert in those sections of the Shulchan Aruch which deal with these questions. To be sure, a Rav Moreh Hora'ah is expected to be proficient in all of the Shulchan Aruch, but there are Rabbanim who have specialized in this particular field, and they are competent to rule whether this or that practice has any suspicion of A. Z. And there is surely no need to emphasize how strictly one must regard any suspicion of A. Z., even the remotest.

In these days of confusion and misconception, additional precaution must be taken to avoid anything, however innocent in itself — if it can be misconstrued by a patient or by a colleague as a **Hetter** for similar treatment or methods which may not be just as innocent of A. Z.

I must emphasize again that the above is no reflection in any way on the Torah knowledge and commitment of any person. But because no person can be fully objective in a matter in which one is personally involved, especially if it is a dedicated involvement, it is important to seek the opinion of a completely objective and disinterested Rabbinic authority.

With blessing for Hatzlocho in all above,

P. S. In view of your writing that you plan to return to Eretz Yisroel soon, this letter has been written ahead of its time.

Enclosed is a copy of a letter which has a bearing on the subject.

The following is a compilation of letters related to meditation that were available to RebbeResonsa.com.

Letter 5

Jewish Meditation and Zen

By the Grace of G-d[91]

9th of Kislev, 5741

Brooklyn, N.Y.

Dr...... P.H.D.

Great Neck, N.Y. 11021

Blessing and Greeting:

This is to acknowledge receipt of your letter of . . ., in which you write about Jewish meditation and "Zen."

Needless to say, your enthusiasm for the latter astonishes me greatly, all the more in view of your introducing yourself as a Ph.D. humanistic psychologist, and having had discussions with knowledgeable Rabbis – which reveals a search for the truth, but regrettably misdirected.

To state some of the reasons for my astonishment, let me, first of all, point out that one of the basic scientific methods is to proceed from the simple to the complex, looking first for simple explanations, and failing to find such, to search for a more complex one. In psychology, too, the first approach should be to relate the problem to the subject's natural element and atmosphere in which he was born, since this has a very strong impact on the person's psyche, for a disturbance or disruption of one's natural element and environment is most likely to be the primary cause of the psychological problem of the patient.

---

91. The Letter and the Spirit, vol. 2, pp. 431ff.

Note: The following letters, which are printed in *"The Letters and the Spirit"* are from the archives of Rabbi Nissan Mindel A"H, the Rebbe's personal secretary entrusted with writing up the Rebbe's orally dictated responses. The "Nissan Mindel Archives" are comprised of secretarial copies, including first drafts, and may have subsequently been published with editorial changes. Therefore the letters as they appear in the book may not be the final signed version.

A second basic point is that the treatment should, of course, be fully consistent with the proper diagnosis, without being subjectively detracted by any method that may seem effective in other circumstances. By way of a simple example: When a drug is prescribed, it should be based entirely on its effectiveness, not by the attractiveness of the pill for its appearance or taste.

A little more deeply. One should not be carried away by immediate but short-lived effects that may be achieved from relieving symptoms, but look for a true and lasting cure, however important it is also to relieve symptoms.

After these prefatory remarks, which are no doubt superfluous in your case, it surprises me that in mentioning your personal background and qualifications, you did not indicate at all how many years you have devoted to in-depth study of the psychological approach expounded in Jewish sources, by Jewish authorities on the subject of guiding Jewish perplexed in every generation. (Some of such sources are available also in translation in various languages).

Moreover, these studies and conclusions have not remained in the realm of theory, but have been tested and proven over the years. For, as in the case of all science, it is actual testing and experimentation that are conclusive, and the more of these, the stronger is the evidence.

Now, although your letter does not indicate that you have had this preparation, either in theory or in practice, which is indispensable in treating Jewish patients with psychological problems, yet you come out with categorical conclusions as to how to treat Jewish patients and, more astonishingly, with the aid of Zen practice at that!

Apparently you are unaware that Zen, as commonly practiced now, is connected with Avoda Zara (idolatry). To be sure, some pagan practices, witchcraft and the like as had been practiced since ancient times, have had palliative effects, by using for example, incense, rhythmical bodily movements and the like, which in the way that tranquilizers nowadays are used as palliatives. Nevertheless, the Torah, **Toras Chaim** and Toras Emes being our true guide in life, strictly prohibits pagan methods and practices insofar as Jews are concerned. And this is because not only will such practices be of no benefit for the soul or body, but will rather be destructive to both – just as there are many "pleasant" substances which also have palliative ingredients but, nonetheless, the total effect is poison. Indeed, it is precisely the external side effects and relief which such practices may bring that cover up the insidious harm and makes them all the more dangerous.

It is surely unnecessary to point out that the purpose of this letter is not polemical. But it is the duty of every human being, certainly of a Jew who follows the teachings of the Torah, to warn any person against pitfalls and help save him, or her, from harm. Since I am a firm believer in G-d's benevolent Providence, as well as in the teaching of our Sages that the heart of every Jew is always awake and responsive to the truth,[92] I trust you will accept what has been said here in the true spirit, and will diligently apply yourself to the study of Jewish sources on the subject of the Jewish soul and psychological make-up. And then, I am confident, you will "taste and see"[93] – to quote a familiar phrase from Tehillim. And by using the proper approach, you will indeed be able to utilize your qualifications and capacities in the fullest measure, to help many who are suffering from confusion and perplexity in these difficult times.

As a young, energetic scientist, who has shown a capacity for research and endurance in the quest for professional excellence, as is evident from your letter, I trust you will accept the new direction I am suggesting to you as a challenge, and I am confident that you will prove equal to it. All the more so as we have the assurance of our Sages, "Make the effort and you will succeed,"[94] coupled with the promise of Divine help.

Wishing you Hatzlocho,

With blessing,

92. See Shir HaShirim 5:2 and Shir HaShirim Rabbah on that verse.

93. *Tehillim* 34:9.

94. Megillah 6b.

Letter 6

Seeking Yoga and Other Cults

By the Grace of G-d[95]

Rosh Chodesh Sivan, 5739

Brooklyn, N.Y.

Mr. . . .

Johannesburg 2000

Greeting and Blessing:

This is to confirm receipt of your letter and may G-d grant the fulfillment of your heart's desires for good.

Noting the beginning of your letter, it is surely unnecessary to reiterate that the everyday life and conduct in accordance with the Torah and mitzvot, although a must for its own sake, is also the channel to receive G-d's blessings in all needs. Consequently, every additional effort in matters of Yiddishkeit widens the channel, and there is always room for improvement in goodness and holiness, Torah and mitzvot.

Referring to the matter of a Jewish name, you are, of course, right that it has a special significance and is incomparable to a name in any other language. However, when it is transliterated — as when a letter is written in English and the name is transliterated in English letters — the original content of the name is preserved, and there can be no objection to it. Besides, there would be no point in signing an English letter in Hebrew, since the recipient may not be able to read Hebrew, which is why the letter is written in English in the first place, in reply to a letter in that language.

Since you brought up this subject, it gives me an opportunity to relate it to the timely topic of these days of sefirah, linking the Festival of Yetzias Mitzraim with the Festival of Mattan Torah. For, as you may know, our Sages declare that one of the things in the merit of which the Jewish people merited the Liberation from Mitzraim was the fact that they did not change their Hebrew names which was an important factor in preserving their identity.[96] Which also reminds us that the ultimate purpose of the liberation from Egyptian bondage was to receive the Torah at Mount Sinai, which we will soon celebrate on Shovuos. With the giving of the Torah, every Jew was given also the capacity, and hence is also fully expected, to go from strength to strength in the study of the Torah and the observance of the mitzvot, bearing in mind that the actual practice is the essential thing.[97]

Inasmuch as the Torah and mitzvot were given to all the Jews, and to each one individually, for all times and in all places, and "these are our lives and the length of our days,"[98] it is clear that every moment of a Jew's life should be consecrated to Torah and mitzvot. Hence it is both surprising and painful to see a Jew spending precious time in search of "greener pastures" elsewhere, even if his intentions are good, for, as above, the important thing is the actual deed.

Needless to say, the above includes **Yoga and similar cults** even if it is not connected with anything pertaining to avodo zoro – if there is such cult that is completely free from avodo zoro, and in this only a competent Torah authority who is permeated with halocho is qualified to rule.

I am not seeking opportunities to admonish anyone, but since you mention certain oriental cults, it is my duty to call your attention to the fact that every spare moment that a Jew can use to deepen his knowledge of Torah he dissipates it on other things is deplorable enough, not to mention cults that in their overwhelming majority are certainly connected with avodo zoro in one way or another, and if there are exceptions, one must make doubly sure through an expert Torah authority, as mentioned above.

The present days are highly suitable for Jews to separate themselves from any alien influences for the Festival of Mattan Toraseinu, when G-d sanctified us as a nation apart from all other nations, a unique "Kingdom of G-d's servants and a Holy Nation,"[99] by giving us His holy Torah and mitzvot. And since G-d Himself has shown us the way, what sense is there in looking for better ways. This is really too plain and self evident to need further elaboration.

Wishing you a joyous and inspiring Festival of Kabbolas haTorah and the traditional blessing to reaffirm the commitment to Torah and mitzvot with joy and inwardness.

With blessing,

95. The Letter and the Spirit, vol. 2, pp. 422ff.

96. See Vayikra Rabbah 32:5.

97. See *Avos* 1:17.

98. Nusach of the evening prayers.

99. *Shemos* 19:6.

Letter 7

Saving Jews from Cults

... I would be remiss if I were not to make the following practical observation. No doubt you know the situation of Yiddishkeit and the problem of assimilation and intermarriage, etc. You must also know of the proliferation of various cults, many of which are definitely idolatrous, which have ensnared many young Jews, both men and women. Many of these cults are also very active in London itself, and their activities are open and public, etc. Sad to say, there has not been an adequate response on the part of Jewish askonim to counter this destructive influence. Even to save one Jewish boy or girl would have warranted the utmost reaction, how much more so when the problem has assumed tidal proportions...

Excerpt from a letter dated 9th of Tammuz, 5740[100]

---

100. The Letter and the Spirit, Vol 3, pp. 447ff.

Letter 8

Nothing is Being Done to Stop Cults Even After a Public Outcry

. . . In recent years a new plague has been ravaging and spreading among our young generation – the various idolatrous "cults." Sad to say, little, if anything has been done to counteract this terrible danger, even after the suicide and loud, but short-lived, outcry in the press. . .

Excerpt from a letter dated 11th of Tishrei, 5741[101]

---

101. *The Letter and the Spirit*, vol. 5, pp. 445ff. It seems that this letter was addressed to Professor Cyril Domb.

Letter 9

Can I Find My Own Way In Life[102]

By the Grace of G-d

28th of Av, 5740

Brooklyn, NY

Miss . . .

Montreal, Que. H3Z 2P8

Canada

Blessing and Greeting:

I am in receipt of your letter and may G-d grant the fulfillment of your heart's desires for the good.

With regard to the question of seeing the true way of life, etc., and your asking me if there is anything wrong for a man or a woman to find his or her own way – this is a surprising question, since the true way of life for a Jew has been set and shown and explained in the Torah, Toras Chaim, by which our people has lived ever since it was given us at Sinai. Seeing that you live in a city where there are many Rabbis and spiritual leaders who can explain to you what this Jewish way of life is, it would certainly be wrong to go searching in darkness.

Of course, there is a special satisfaction in finding things out for oneself, but this is a case similar to a situation where a person would say that he will stop eating and drinking until he finds out for himself how food and water sustains one's health; or the case of a person who, ignoring warnings that certain foods are harmful or poisonous, will nevertheless decide to indulge himself freely, until he finds out for himself. It would certainly be very wrong and illogical not to rely on authorities and experts in those areas, to which they had dedicated most of their life, study and research, claiming the right of man or woman, to find his or her own way. What is true of physical health is also true of spiritual health and with even more far-reaching consequences.

The above goes for all Jewish young men and women who go out searching for the truth in various cults, yoga and mystical philosophy where they are sure to find out sooner or later that they have been wasting their precious time and life in searching for the truth which has been right before their eyes all along in the Torah, Toras Emes. They are wrong also in thinking that since it is their own life, they can do what they like with it, for life has been given by the giver of Life to be lived in accordance with the way He set forth in His Torah and not to experiment with it recklessly, etc.

Much more could be said on the subject, but the above lines should suffice.

In summary, regardless of how you conducted yourself in the past, or what your approach has been, you ought to lose no time in ordering your life in strict accord with the Shulchan Aruch, and later on having the benefit of such an everyday life of mitzvos, the performance of which in itself deepens one's perception and insights, and having fortified your starving soul, if you will desire to learn more about the deeper meaning and aspects of the mitzvos, you could do so under the guidance of one who personifies this kind of life and is an authority on the subject. To argue about one's "right" in this situation, would be like a fish arguing that no one has a right to compel it to stay in the water if it wants to jump out of it on dry land and find out for itself what it would be like to live outside its natural element, and then it would decide what to do.[103]

With blessing,

---

102. The Letter and the Spirit, Vol 5, pp. 233ff.

103. See *Berachos* 61b.

Letter 10 (two letters)

Meditation as Therapy

Greeting and Blessing:

[...] I am gratified to read about your advancement in matters of Yiddishekeit, where there is always room for improvement, since all matters of goodness and holiness, Torah and Mitzvoth, are infinite, being connected with the Infinite. Although this is a must for its own sake, this is also the way to receive additional blessings in all needs...

You mention the matter of meditation as a therapeutic technique, but you do not mention the details involved, and perhaps you are not aware of the details. At any rate, I trust you know that this technique is often associated with certain cults which are strictly forbidden by the Torah. Therefore you should discuss the matter with a competent Rabbi to make sure that nothing is involved there that is contrary to the Torah.

With blessing,

(Excerpts from a letter to Mr. D..

dated 14 Tammuz. 5738)

Greeting and Blessing:

This is to acknowledge receipt of your letter of the 28th of Shevat, in which you write that you are keeping in touch with your Chabad friends in London, and are consulting with them. You will no doubt continue to do so, and will surely be able to find the proper solutions to various matters, as it is written, "Help comes with the abundance of counsel."

With reference to the school that you mention, I believe I already indicated to you that as long as you have no complete Hetter from Chief Rabbi Jakobovits, it is the proper thing for you to have withdrawn from it.

I am confident that with contemplation on matters of Kedusha and Tefilla, coupled with regular Shiurim in Torah, which I was pleased to note from your letter, and which I trust you will increase steadily, you will make considerable strides in all matters of Yiddishkeit, in peace of mind and general good health, especially in preparation for your marriage.

Now that we are in the month of Adar, the month of increased joy, highlighted by Purim, when there was "Light, Joy, Gladness and Honor" for all Jews, may this be so for you in every respect, materially and spiritually.

With best wishes for a joyous and inspiring Purim, With blessing, [the Rebbe's signature]

(a letter to Mr. D.. dated 6 Adar. 5739)

Letter 11

Questions on Meditation

By the Grace of G-d[104]

4th of Elul, 5731

Brooklyn, N.Y.

Mr. . . .

Bronx, N.Y. 10451

Greeting and Blessing:

Your letter reached me with considerable delay. In it you write about your practice of meditation, etc., and you ask elucidation on a number of religious questions.

It is, of course, difficult to explain such matters adequately in a letter. However, I might mention a general principle which, as many aspects of the Torah, are expressed in a few concise words. I am referring to the expression "Torah-Or." This means that one of the primary functions of the Torah is to illuminate everything in its true light. For such is the function of light in general, since in the absence of it there is darkness and in darkness a person can only grope and feel, and rely on the sense of touch, which is of course very unreliable. It is possible, for example, to mistake a very valuable gem for an ordinary piece of glass, or vice versa.

Similarly in the daily life, when a person seeks true meaning in life involving both the emotions and intellect it is possible for a Jew to find a meaningful life only in the Torah, and in its directives and guidance.

In light of the above, when you write about meditation, the important thing is what the meditation is on, and what the meditation leads to. Here again the Torah has its clear say on meditation, when it is to be practiced and what its content should be. The Torah tells us that meditation should be before prayer as a preparation to attune one's mind and heart to G-d, and that the meditation should be on the exaltedness and majesty of G-d and on the smallness and insignificance of man. In other words, to help a person realize that the material and physical aspects in life are not an end in themselves, but must be made subservient to the spiritual, holy and G-dly. And having thus elevated himself through meditation itself and through the prayer itself, the Jew can then go on to implement these truths in his actual daily life and conduct. As to the question how much time should be devoted to meditation and introspection, this, of course depends on the individual, his character and frame of mind in each particular day, etc. All this is clearly spelled out in the Shulchan Aruch (Orach Chaim, beg. 98 See it there.)

Needless to say, as in everything else, G-d's help is needed also in this, and one of the good practices in this connection is to set aside a small coin for tzedoko every weekday morning before prayer.

It is superfluous to emphasize that what you write about the nature of meditation does not at all correspond to what has been said above.

Another important point that I wish to make, is also at variance with what you write. I refer to the fact that according to our Torah, Torah Or, the important thing is the deed. As a matter of fact, the deed, namely the actual fulfillment of the Torah and mitzvot in the daily life, is the primary objective, and it is through actual practice of the Torah and mitzvot that a Jew obtains a deeper insight into their meaning and significance.

The way to such meditation as mentioned above is through the study of those sections in Torah (Mussar and Chasidus), where the subject matter is discussed.

With regard to the question of **diet**, here too we have clear directives in the Torah as to what a Jew is permitted and not permitted to include in his diet. It is self evident that the nourishment which a person consumes is directly related also not only to his physical but also to his mental faculties. But we also have a clear directive in the Torah that a Jew is permitted to eat meat, and need not restrict his diet to vegetarian food.1 The thing is that the meat has to be kosher in every respect. As a matter of fact, on Shabbos and Yom Tov, the eating of meat has a special significance.

A further point, which has been mentioned above in passing, should be emphasized. It is that the daily conduct in accordance with Torah, the actual fulfillment of the mitzvot in the daily life and the religious experience itself, have the effect of refining the general character of the individual, both his emotional as well as his thoughts, and make him more receptive to understand his life and his purpose in life, etc.. This too may be found in the ethical and Chasidic teachings, which are part of the Torah.

Finally, inasmuch as you are a college student, I will offer an analogy from the world of science. A person who wishes to make a study of any particular subject in the world of science, has before him two options: a) He may wish to start from scratch independently, or b) He may familiarize himself with what has already been discovered and attained by others who preceded him, and, instead of trying to verify all that for himself, utilizes his time and efforts to make further advancement. The first method has two obvious disadvantages 1) It is first of all a waste of time, inasmuch as others have already done all the exploration and investigation and have finally reached their conclusions. 2) No less important is also the consideration that it is very possible that his independent studies may altogether prove futile, or worse still, may lead him to make false deductions. On the other hand, if he accepts the body of knowledge and experience of previous generations, and conclusions arrived at by specialists and authorities, he is certain to be on the right track.

The above is true also in regard to meditation and the whole approach to finding one's way in life. There is living proof that does not even require any faith, to the effect that the survival of the Jewish people since its inception more than 3,000 years ago, is due only to Jewish adherence to the Jewish way of life, in accordance with the Torah and mitzvot. Be it remembered that throughout this long period of history, the Jewish people have been put to various tests, and through various "experiments" such as all sorts of persecutions, wars and other crises, yet the Jewish people has outlived the mighty nations and empires of the world who had attempted to annihilate the small Jewish nation. The only single factor that helped the Jewish people survive and overcome its adversaries and to preserve its identity and uniqueness, has not been a language, or territory but the adherence to the Torah and mitzvot in its totality, with the observance of Shabbos, kashrus, the putting on of tefillin and the practice of other mitzvot, as commanded in the Written Torah and explained in detail in the Oral Torah.

I trust it is unnecessary to elaborate further on the above to you. May G-d grant that you should accept the directives of the Torah as a guide in life and way of life in the same spirit as when it was given at Sinai, when the Jewish people accepted the Torah on the principle of naaseh (we will do), and then v'nishma (we will understand). One must not expect to understand everything right away, since there is a body of knowledge which has accumulated over forty generations, and it still cannot be fully fathomed. But, as mentioned above, the proper approach is to begin with the practice of the mitzvot, since that in itself refines the mind and heart, and provides the insights into the deeper meaning. May you also be a living example in your environment as to how a Jew should live his daily life, in accordance with the Torah, called Toras Chaim and mitzvot by which Jews live. In the final analysis it is primarily a matter of one's own will and determination.

Wishing you hatzlocho and a Kasivo vaChasimo Tovo,

With blessing,

---

104. *The Letter and the Spirit*, Vol. 2, pp. 161ff.

Letter 12

Using LSD for Mystical Inspiration

By the Grace of G-d,
20th of Marcheshvan, 5725
[Oct. 26, 1964]
Brooklyn, N.Y.

Greeting and Blessings:

I am in receipt of your letter of October 18th, which you write in the name of your friends and in your own behalf, and ask my opinion regarding the new drug called L.S.D., which is said to have the property of mental stimulation, etc.

Biochemistry is not my field, and I cannot express an opinion on the drug you mention, especially as it is still new. However what I can say is that the claim that the said drug can stimulate mystical insight, etc., is not the proper way to attain mystical inspiration, even *if* it had such a property. The Jewish way is to go from strength to strength, not by means of drugs and other artificial stimulants, which have a place only if they are necessary for the physical health, in accordance with the Mitzva to take care of one's health. I hope that everyone will agree that before any drugs are taken one should first utilize all one's natural capacities, and when this is done *truly and fully*, I do not think there will be a need to look for artificial stimulants.

I trust that you and your group, in view of your Yeshiva background, have regular appointed times for the study of Torah, and the inner aspects of the Torah, namely the teachings of Chassidus, and that such study is in accordance with the principle of our Sages, namely "The essential thing is the deed," i.e., the actual conduct of the daily life in accordance with the Torah and Mitzvoth, prayer, Tefillin, Kashruth, etc., etc. This is only a matter of will and determination, for nothing stands in the way of the will. I trust that you are also using your good influence throughout your environment.

With blessing,

Transcription of the 13 Tammuz, 5739 (July 8, 1979) talk on kosher meditation

(https://www.chabad.org/therebbe/article_cdo/aid/2601787/jewish/13th-Day-of-Tammuz-5739-1979.htm)

(5). There in an issue, which is connected with the physical and psychological health of many Jews, that demands attention. It is quite possible that these words will have no effect. Nevertheless, the health of a Jew is such an important matter, that efforts should be made even when there is not a sure chance of success.

This issue is the idea of meditation. Meditation has its roots in the very beginning of the Jewish heritage. The Torah commentaries explain that Avraham and the other patriarchs chose to be shepherds so that they could spend their time in solitude. Their lives were not simple, physical lives. On the contrary, they were totally given over to the service of G-d to the point where they are called "G-d's chariot." [That metaphor was chosen because just as a chariot has no will of its own and is totally controlled by its driver, similarly their lives were totally controlled by G-d.] They chose a profession that would allow them to live such a spiritual existence. Therefore, they become shepherds, spending their days in the fields, in solitude, rather than becoming involved in the hub-bub of life in the cities.

The same holds true today. There are certain aspects of psychological health and tranquility that can be attained by taking oneself out of contact with the hub-bub that surrounds oneself. By retreating into solitude, (not necessary leaving the city,) and by withdrawing into solitude for a period of time, one may attain psychological health and peace of mind. This behavior will strengthen one and protect his mental health. This process involves taking oneself away from the hub-bub and tumult of the street, and meditating on an object that brings about peace of mind.

The Torah's statement "Behold I have set before you life and good, death and evil" applies in all matters. Every facet of life can be used in a positive way or in an opposite direction. For example, the sun, the moon, and the stars are necessary for life of earth. They bring about manifold goodness. However, they also have been worshipped as false gods. One might ask (as the Talmud asks): "Since they have been worshipped as false gods, shouldn't they be destroyed? However, should G-d destroy the world because of the foolishness of the idol-worshipers?" The same concept applies in regard to meditation. Though essentially good, meditation can also be destructive. There are those who have connected meditation to actually bowing down to an idol or a man and worshipping it or him, bringing incense before them etc. The cults have spread throughout the U.S. and throughout Israel as well. They have called it by a refined name "transcendental meditation" i.e. something above limits, above our bounded intellects. However, they have also incorporated into the procedures the bringing of incense and other practices that are clearly "Avodah Zara," the worship of false gods.

Since we are living within the darkness of Golus, many Jewish youth have fallen into this snare. Before they became involved with this cult, they were troubled and disturbed. The cult was able to relate to them and bring them peace of mind. However, their meditation is connected with Avodah Zara, burning incense and bowing to a Guru, etc. Since the aspects of idol worship are not publicized, there are those who have not raised their voices in protest. They don't know if such a protest would be successful and since no one has asked them, why should they enter a questionable situation. However, while they remain silent, Jewish youth are becoming involved in "Avodah Zara," worship of idols. That sin is so severe that the Torah declares one should forego his life before accepting their worship. Furthermore, this plague is spreading, involving both youth and adults alike.[11]

A program must be organized to spread Kosher meditation. There are those who argue against such a step. They question its propriety maintaining that Kosher meditation might lead to non-Kosher meditation. Their argument can be refuted. It is opposite the spirit of Yiddishkeit, and particularly opposite the spirit of Chassidus, to withhold help from anyone. If someone is in need, one must help him. If someone does not realize that he requires help, the need to help him is even greater.

However, that is not the question at all. There are Jews who have already fallen into this snare. The simplest way to draw them away from it would be to provide them with a Kosher alternative. We are clearly obligated from the Torah to do so.[12] (If not as a Mitzvah in its own right as a part of the Mitzvah "love your neighbor as yourself.")

Others will argue — such a practice will lead to "Bitul Torah, the neglect of Torah study." Since many of those who will seek meditation are not involved in a Torah lifestyle, the concepts that relax them and put them at ease when meditating are not necessarily connected with Torah. Though a Kosher topic of meditation will be chosen, it will not necessarily be connected with Torah. Hence, such a practice causes a neglect of Torah study.

This argument is also faulty. These people are sick and must be healed. They should be given a Kosher method of treatment instead of being forced to use means that are connected with Avodah Zara.

Two conditions must be taken into consideration: 1) meditation should only be used by those who need it. A healthy person doesn't need meditation. On the contrary, if he begins to meditate he will hurt his psychological health.[13] The only meditation that all should carry out is one which is part of one's service to G-d, for the *Shulchan Aruch* states that before each prayer one must meditate on "the greatness of G-d and the humble state of man." However, that meditation is done with a fixed time and a fixed intent. Its goal is not to calm one's nerves. 2) The meditation must be based on a Kosher idea or a Torah concept e.g. Shema Yisroel, the meanings of the prayers. Thus, this will bring one to an awareness of the greatness of G-d and the humble nature of man.

Also, since as in all treatments, the healer gains a certain amount of control over his patient, we must take care that the professional who is leading the meditation have a clear and well defined knowledge of what is permitted according to the *Shulchan Aruch,* what leads to Avodah Zara, etc.

In addition, the professional must be conscious that meditation shares a parallel with other medical remedies. Drugs and medicines are only valuable if given in a limited amount, and are detrimental to one's health if taken overexcessively. Someone, who is dangerously ill should take meditation in order to be cured. However, once he is cured, to persist in taking the remedy is harmful. Similarly, in regard to meditation, the measure in which a person is exposed to it must be regulated. This principle is expressed by the Rambam who writes, that if someone is overindulgent in a certain direction he will be healed by taking extreme steps in the opposite direction. However, after the influence of his initial behavior has been counteracted, he should return to a middle path.

There are general guidelines for establishing a program of Kosher meditation. It is necessary that we do not close our eyes and return to our daily lives, thinking, what does meditation have to do with me? What contact do I share with the youth and adults that have fallen into this snare? We must realize that there are many in the United States, who have become involved. In Israel, many centers for meditation have been opened. Even in Yerushalayim, the holy city, such a center has been established. I, myself, received a brochure from such an institution. It was professionally produced, containing pictures and a description of how in Yerushalayim, a center for meditation has been set up. They purchase American addresses, and send them this brochure. It makes a powerful impression and arouses curiosity. Thus, we can see how serious the situation is.

In view of this situation, psychologists, psychoanalysts, etc. have a holy duty to advance their knowledge of meditation, and work to develop a Kosher program. Furthermore, since we live in a country in which publicity plays a large role, efforts must be made to publicize the treatment in the broadest means possible.

Furthermore, this treatment should not be connected with any side issues. There are those who maintain that meditation must be connected with the secrets of Torah. Meditation on the secrets of Torah is very important, particularly in the present age when the Wellsprings of Chassidus must be spread outwards. However, the subject at hand is different. There are Jews who are involved in "Avodah Zara," worship of false gods, who must be saved. This is the first priority. If one begins by teaching the secrets of Torah, it is extremely likely that the majority of them will not respond. Even the few who might show an interest should be separated from "Avodah Zara" first.

It is a necessity for everyone to be involved in this. However, if a novice would begin learning meditation immediately, it would take a long time before he could master the subject. Instead, one should turn to a psychologist and attempt to interest him in the matter. He should be told that thousands of Jews are being drawn into the worship of idols, bringing incense, believing in Gurus, etc., and how he has a holy duty (and since he also has a personal desire) to heal people, it is necessary that he extend himself into a field related to his own — meditation. In a short time, he will be able to master the techniques necessary for this treatment, since he already has had practical experience helping such people.

This aspect, if publicized correctly, will be immediately successful. It will be able to save those who stand at the crossroads. Their intent is not against Torah. If given the choice between a permitted treatment and a forbidden one, they will choose the permitted. Then, this success, will attract those who have already become involved with the forbidden practices.

We cannot sit and wait practically until someone asks to be helped. We have to approach those who are afflicted and speak their language, without mixing in any other Mitzvos. Our object should be merely the Mitzvah of healing their troubled psyches.

Each one of us knows such a doctor. We can interest a doctor in such activities, and he will find a way to attract those who have fallen into these snares.

These efforts are most important. Our sages declared: "One who saves a Jewish soul saves the entire world." In this case, there are thousands of souls that must be saved. There will be critics. However, the very first chapter of *Shulchan Aruch* opens with the command "Don't be embarrassed before those who mock you." Rather than be affected by these doubts, we can proudly save many Jewish souls returning them to their source; sound in mind, and sound in body.

And then, through this effort of saving Jewish souls we will proceed to the future redemption. In all the other exiles, the redemption did not involve the entire Jewish people. However, the Messianic redemption will reach every Jew. The prophet Isaiah (27:12) declares: "You will be collected one by one" from Even the furthest extremes of Golus. These efforts to draw Jews away from the Golus of "Avodah Zara" will help hasten the fulfillment of the prophecy. The Talmud states that all the appointed times for Moshiach's coming have passed, and everything depends on Teshuvah. When the Jewish people do Teshuvah, they will immediately be redeemed.

11. The pattern "one sin leads to another" will bring those who have not been involved with the aspects of meditation that are Avodah Zara to this severe sin. Once they have begun meditation they will look for a greater Guru and a more well known Guru until they fall into that snare.

12. Also, by doing so we will fulfill the Mitzvah of healing a fellow Jew.

13. A parallel to this idea can be seen in the Talmud. Our sages declared that the workers of Mechuzah who were used to carrying heavy loads would become sick if they did not work. Likewise, those who don't need to take time off and relax will suffer by doing so.

Appendix B: Information for Healthcare Providers

If you are starting meditation to address an existing health issue, please share this information with your healthcare provider.

The meditation recommended in this book is adapted from practices that patients and the general public have used for over 60 years. Instructions allow for individualized technique adjustment and self-regulation. Research confirms meditation's clinical value as an adjunct to standard medical treatment for various conditions, including hypertension, coronary artery disease, insomnia, addiction, asthma, epilepsy, hypercholesterolemia, diabetes, psoriasis, and fibromyalgia. Well-documented benefits of regular meditation practice include stress reduction and an overall improvement in well-being.

The recommended time frame is 20 minutes or less, twice a day. Although rare, serious side-effects have been reported, but mostly for people who have significantly increased the time and frequency of meditation. Often, there is a preexisting condition that may have been exacerbated by meditation.

To reduce the experience of side effects are instructions to reduce the time in meditation, and to stop altogether if meditation becomes uncomfortable.

Special Patient Populations: Managing Risks

Hypertension

While meditation generally helps reduce blood pressure, occasional paradoxical increases have been reported with other relaxation techniques. Monitor hypertensive patients' blood pressure regularly during their first 90 days of meditation practice. If significant increases occur, advise discontinuation of the practice.

Diabetes

Deep relaxation may impact insulin requirements and lead to hypoglycemia. Advise diabetic patients to frequently monitor urinary glucose levels and keep a readily absorbable glucose supply available. Adjustments to medication or diet may be necessary.

Thyroidectomized patients

Deep relaxation has triggered hyperthyroidism symptoms in some thyroidectomized patients. Start these patients with short meditation periods (three minutes, two to three times daily) and monitor their condition for two weeks. Gradually increase meditation time if they remain asymptomatic.

Medication effects

Meditation may enhance the action of anti-anxiety, anti-depressive, anti-hypertensive, and thyroid-regulating drugs. Monitor patients' medication requirements, as continued meditation practice may allow for lower dosages or discontinuation of drug therapy.

Physician support

Your encouragement of patients' meditation practice, particularly for hypertensive patients, can greatly improve compliance and benefits. Regularly inquire about their practice, offer guidance, and acknowledge progress.

Contraindications

While meditation is generally safe, it may not be suitable for patients with severe mental illness (e.g., schizophrenia, bipolar disorder), patients on anti-psychotic medications, and those experiencing significant emotional distress. Use discretion when recommending for these populations.

Severe PTSD requires special consideration. While preliminary research suggests meditation could be a beneficial intervention, it's crucial to approach with caution. As the mind settles, extremely intense traumatic memories may emerge. Close supervision by a skilled healthcare provider is essential to help the client navigate these potentially distressing experiences.

Glossary

Nisan, Iyar, Sivan, Tamuz, Av, Elul, Tishrei, Marheshvan, Kislev, Tevet, Shevat, Adar I, Adar II: Months of the Jewish Calendar

Avodah Zarah: A Hebrew term for idolatry or the worship of false gods.

Pirkei Avot: A tractate of the Mishnah that focuses on ethics and the transmission of the Oral Torah.

Beit refuah: A Hebrew term for "house of healing," over the Israeli use of **beit cholim**, meaning "house of the sick," for hospitals.

Bitul Torah: The neglect of Torah study.

Chabad: A movement within the Chassidic branch of Judaism. The name is an acronym for Chochmah, Binah, Da'at, which are the three terms in Kabbalah that represent the three primary aspects of scholarship: wisdom (Chochmah), understanding (Binah), and knowledge (Da'at).

Chalutzah: Pioneer.

Chassidus: Chassidic (or Hasidic) movement within Judaism

Chedvah: A Hebrew word that refers to the four-letter name of G-d.

Cheshvan: A shortened form of the name of the second month of the Hebrew calendar.

Chodesh: Month (Yiddish).

Devarim: The fifth book of the Torah, also known as Deuteronomy.

Echod: The Hebrew word for "one." It's suggested as a potential focus word for meditation, reflecting the Jewish principle of G-d's unity.

Elokeinu: A Hebrew word that means "our G-d."

Elul: The twelfth month of the Hebrew calendar.

Eretz Yisroel: The Hebrew term for the land of Israel.

Farbrengen: A gathering or celebration, especially a festive gathering of Chassidim.

G-d: G-d (Hebrew); the dash is a common convention in Jewish writing to avoid writing the name in full.

Golus: The Hebrew word for "exile" or "diaspora." It refers to the dispersion of the Jews outside the land of Israel.

Halachically: Relating to Halakha, the collective body of Jewish religious laws derived from the written and oral Torah.

Hashem: A Hebrew word that means "the Name" and is used as a substitute for the four-letter name of G-d in order to avoid taking the name in vain.

Hasid (also **Chassid**): A devout and pious person.

Hisbonenus: Contemplation (Hebrew); a type of Jewish meditation.

Hitbodedut: Means "self-seclusion" or "solitude." A type of unstructured, spontaneous, and individualized prayer and meditation popularized by Rabbi Nachman of Breslov.

Hisbonenus: Is an active thought-meditation practice that focuses on deep intellectual contemplation.

Kabbalah: A body of mystical Jewish teachings based on an esoteric interpretation of the Hebrew Scriptures.

Kabbalistic: Relating to Kabbalah, a school of Jewish mysticism.

Keter: A Hebrew word that means "crown."

Kosher: A Hebrew word that means "fit" or "proper." In the context of food, it refers to the dietary standards of traditional Jewish law, but in this book, it's used to describe a form of meditation that is acceptable according to Jewish principles, free from idolatrous or non-Jewish religious elements.

Lubavitcher: A follower of the Lubavitch (Chabad) Chassidic movement.

Malchut: A Hebrew word that means "kingdom."

Mechuzah: A Talmudic term, workers of Mechuzah were those who carried heavy loads.

Mitzvah: A singular commandment or law in Judaism.

Moshiach: The Hebrew word for "Messiah," the anointed one. In Judaism, Moshiach is the future king of the Jewish people who will redeem the Jews and bring peace and prosperity to the entire world.

Orach Chayim: A section of the Shulchan Aruch, focused on the laws of prayer and the grace after meals.

Pikuach Nefesh: A Hebrew term meaning "saving a life," which in Jewish law refers to the principle that preserving human life takes precedence over nearly all other religious obligations.

Rambam: Rabbi Moshe ben Maimon, a preeminent medieval Sephardic Jewish philosopher and physician.

Rashi: An acronym for Rabbi Shlomo Yitzchaki, a renowned medieval French commentator on the Hebrew Bible and the Talmud.

Rebbe: Rabbi (Yiddish); a title of respect used to address a leader of a Chassidic dynasty.

Sefer Yetzirah: Translated as the Book of Creation or the Book of Formation, is a foundational text of Jewish mysticism, possibly the earliest work of Kabbalistic thought.

Sephardic: Relating to Jews of Spanish, Portuguese, or North African descent.

Sh'ma or Shema Yisrael: A Hebrew word that means "hear" or "listen." A central prayer in Judaism, beginning with the words "Hear, O Israel: the Lord our G-d, the Lord is one." The word "Shema" is suggested as a potential focus word for meditation.

Shefa: A Hebrew word that means "abundance" or "flow."

Shulchan Aruch: A code of Jewish law written by Rabbi Yosef Karo in the 16th century. It's considered one of the most authoritative works of halakha (Jewish law).

Sichos Kodesh: Holy discourses or talks.

Talmud: A central text of Rabbinic Judaism. It is a record of Jewish oral law and consists of the Mishnah and the Gemara.

Talmud Torah: A Jewish day school or afternoon school for religious studies.

Tanya: A foundational text of the Chabad Chassidic movement.

Tefillin: A set of black leather boxes containing scrolls of parchment inscribed with verses from the Torah, worn by Jewish men during weekday morning prayers.

Teshura: A letter or epistle.

Teshuvah: Repentance (Hebrew); a Baal Teshuvah is a term for a Jewish person who becomes more observant Jewish law.

Tzfat: A city in the northern region of Israel. One of three holy cities in Israel.

Yechidus: A private audience with a Rebbe, or Hasidic leader.

Yerushalayim: The Hebrew name for Jerusalem.

Yom Tov: Good holiday (Hebrew); a greeting used on holidays.

Zechus Harabim: A Hebrew term meaning "the merit of the rabbis," referring to the concept that the virtuous deeds of the rabbis benefit the community.

Zohar: A foundational text of Jewish mysticism, often used in Kabbalistic studies and meditation.

Notes

Introduction

1. American Psychological Association. 2022. "Stress in America: Concerned for the Future, Battered by Inflation." Retrieved from https://www.apa.org/news/press/releases/stress/2022/concerned-future-inflation.
2. Adini, B., et al. 2020. "Depression and Anxiety Rates Rise Significantly during COVID-19 Pandemic." *Tel Aviv University News*. https://english.tau.ac.il/news/depression-covid19.
3. Shmueli, E., et al. 2023. "Post-traumatic Stress Disorder Affects 23% of Adult Jewish Israelis following October 7th Attacks." *medRxiv*. https://www.aftau.org/news_item/tau-research-23-of-adult-jewish-israelis-now-suffer-from-post-traumatic-stress-disorder/.
4. Ghert-Zand, Renee. 2024. "October 7 and War Trauma Will Lead to At Least 30,000 New Cases of PTSD, Expert Says." *The Times of Israel*, 12 Adar I 5784 (February 21, 2024). https://www.timesofisrael.com/october-7-and-war-trauma-will-lead-to-at-least-30000-new-cases-of-ptsd-expert-says/?utm_source=pocket_saves.
5. Gallup. 2024. "Leading Countries/Region Worldwide Based on Stress Experienced in the Previous Day in 2023." *Statista*. Retrieved February 2, 2025, from

https://www.statista.com/statistics/1057961/the-most-stressed-out-populations-worldwide/.

Chapter 1

1. Miller, Chaim. 2014. *Turning Judaism Outward: A Biography of the Rebbe*. Menachem M. Schneerson. New York: Kol Menachem, 5774 [2014]), 347.
2. Letter from the Rebbe to Rabbi Yaakov Landau, 25 Tammuz 5737 (July 11, 1977).
3. Landes, Yehoshua. 2014. "The Inside Story of the Founding of Jewish Meditation." *B'Or Ha'Torah* 23: 171.
4. Doolittle, Mark J. (n.d.) "Stress and Cancer: An Overview." Stanford Medicine. Retrieved January 27, 2025, from https://med.stanford.edu/survivingcancer/cancer-and-stress/stress-and-cancer.html.

Chapter 2

1. Cleveland Clinic. "Stress." Retrieved February 2, 2025, https://my.clevelandclinic.org/health/diseases/11874-stress.

2. Benson, Herbert, and Miriam Z. Klipper. 2001. *Relaxation Response*. New York: Quill, 8–9.

3. Benson and Klipper. *Relaxation Response*, 97.

4. Benson and Klipper. *Relaxation Response*, 97.

5. Benson, Herbert, and William Proctor. 2010. *Relaxation Revolution: The Science and Genetics of Mind Body Healing.* New York: Scribner, chapter 7.

Chapter 3

1. Benson and Klipper. *Relaxation Response*, 8.

2. Avey, Holly, et al. "Health Care Providers' Training, Perceptions, and Practices Regarding Stress and Health Outcomes." *Journal of the National Medical Association* 95, no. 9: 836. PMID: 14527051.

3. Benson and Klipper. *Relaxation Response*, 8.

4. Benson and Klipper. *Relaxation Response*, 108.

5. Benson and Klipper. *Relaxation Response*, 116.

6. Benson and Klipper. *Relaxation Response*, 125.

7. Benson and Klipper. *Relaxation Response*, 126-153

8. Benson and Klipper. *Relaxation Response*, 30.

9. Benson and Proctor. *Relaxation Revolution*, 99–108.

10. Benson and Proctor. *Relaxation Revolution*, 56.

11. Benson, Herbert, Beary, John F., and Carol, Mark P. 1974. "The Relaxation Response." *Psychiatry* 37, no. 1 (February 1974): 37–46. https://doi.org/10.1080/00332747.1974.11023785.

12. Benson and Klipper. *Relaxation Response*, 10.

13. Benson and Klipper. *The Relaxation Response* (25th Anniversary Edition), preface.

14. Benson, Herbert, and Marg Stark. 1996. *Timeless Healing: The Power and Biology of Belief.* New York: Simon and Schuster.

15. Benson and Proctor. *Relaxation Revolution*, 18.

16. Benson and Klipper. *Relaxation Response*, 110–112.

17. Benson and Klipper. *Relaxation Response*, 114.

18. Benson and Klipper. *Relaxation Response*, 116.

19. Stefano, George B., et al. 2001. "The Placebo Effect and Relaxation Response: Neural Processes and Their Coupling to Constitutive Nitric Oxide." *Brain Research Reviews* 35, no. 1 (March): 1–19. https://doi.org/10.1016/S0165-0173(00)00047-3.

20. Dusek, Jeffery A., et al. 2006. "Association between Oxygen Consumption and Nitric Oxide Production during the Relaxation Response." *Medical Science*

Monitor 12, no. 1 (January): CR1–10. Epub December 19, 2005, PMID: 16369463.

21. Lazar, Sara W., et al. 2005. "Meditation Experience Is Associated with Increased Cortical Thickness." *Neuroreport* 16, no. 17 (November 28, 2005): 1893. https://doi.org/10.1097/01.wnr.0000186598.66243.19.

22. Dusek, Jeffery A., et al. 2008. "Genomic Counter-Stress Changes Induced by the Relaxation Response." *PLoS One* 3, no. 7 (July 2, 2008): e2576. https://doi.org/10.1371/journal.pone.0002576.

Chapter 4

1. Excerpted from Sichos Kodesh 5739, Vol.III, p. 314ff.

2. Letter from the Rebbe to Dr. Yehuda Landes, 10 Tammuz, 5739 (June 30, 1979) (see Appendix A, Letter 7).

Chapter 8

1. Farias, M., et al. 2020. "Adverse Events in Meditation Practices and Meditation-Based Therapies: A Systematic Review." *Acta*

Psychiatrica Scandinavica 142, no. 5: 374-393. https://doi.org/10.1111/acps.13225.

2. Lambert, D., van den Berg, N.H., and Mendrek, A. 2023. "Adverse Effects of Meditation: A Review of Observational, Experimental, and Case Studies." *Curr Psychol* 42: 1112–1125.

3. Farias, et al. "Adverse Events in Meditation Practices," 374–393.

4. PACEs Connection. 2018. "Meditation May Aggravate Trauma, Mindful Action Is a Better Alternative." https://www.pacesconnection.com/blog/meditation-may-aggravate-trauma-mindful-action-is-a-better-alternative.

5. Nidich, Sanford, et al. 2018. "Non-Trauma-Focused Meditation Versus Exposure Therapy in Veterans with Post-Traumatic Stress Disorder: A Randomised Controlled Trial." *Lancet Psychiatry* 5, no. 12: 975–986. https://www.thelancet.com/journals/lanpsy/article/PIIS2215-0366(18)30384-5/abstract.

6. Ross, Gina. 2008. *Beyond the Trauma Vortex into the Healing Vortex: A Guide for You.* Los Angeles: The International Trauma-Healing Institute.

Chapter 9

1. Benson and Proctor. *Relaxation Revolution*, 49.

2. Benson and Proctor. *Relaxation Revolution*, 75.

3. Benson and Proctor. *Relaxation Revolution*, 75–76.

4. Benson, Herbert, and Richard Friedman. 1996. "Harnessing the Power of the Placebo Effect and Renaming It 'Remembered Wellness'." *Annual Review of Medicine* 47: 193–9. https://doi.org/10.1146/annurev.med.47.1.193.

5. Solan, Matthew. 2022. "The Real Power of Placebos." Boston: Harvard Health Publishing. https://www.health.harvard.edu/staying-healthy/the-real-power-of-placebos.

6. Lembo, Anthony, et al. 2021. "Open-Label Placebo vs Double-Blind Placebo for Irritable Bowel Syndrome: A Randomized Clinical Trial." *Pain* 162, no. 9 (September 1, 2021): 2428. https://doi.org/10.1097/j.pain.0000000000002234.

7. Rankin, Lissa. 2020. *Mind Over Medicine: Scientific Proof That You Can Heal Yourself.* Carlsbad, California: Hay House, 299.

8. Rankin. Mind Over Medicine, 8.

9. Rankin. Mind Over Medicine, 8–9.

10. Rankin. Mind Over Medicine, 25

11. Benson, Herbert, and William Proctor. 2003. *The Breakout Principle: How to Activate the Natural Trigger That Maximizes Creativity, Athletic Performance, Productivity, and Personal Well-Being.* New York: Scribner, 226.

12. Siegel, Bernie S. 1986. *Love, Medicine & Miracles.* New York: Harper & Row, 133 (referenced in Rankin, *Mind Over Medicine*, 25).

13. Kissel, Pierre, and Dominique Barrucand. 1964. *Placebos et Effet Placebo en Médecine.* Paris: Masson (referenced in Rankin, *Mind Over Medicine*, 25).

Chapter 10

1. Beck, Aaron T., et al. 1979. *Cognitive Therapy of Depression.* New York: Guilford.

2. Freeman, Tzvi. (n.d.). "What Is Bitachon?" *Building Blocks of Jewish Thought* (online library). https://www.chabad.org/library/article_cdo/aid/1405289/jewish/Bitachon.htm.

3. Ibn Pekuda, Rabbeinu Bachya. 2021. *Shaar Habitachon—The Gate of Trust.* New York: Kehot Publication Society & Chayenu.

https://www.chabad.org/library/article_cdo/aid/5478224/jewish/Introduction-Part-1.htm#lt=primary.

4. Kalmenson, Mendel. 2019. *Positivity Bias—Practical Wisdom for Positive Living.* New York: Ezra Press.

5. Kalmenson. *Positivity Bias,* 13.

6. Kalmenson. *Positivity Bias,* 13.

7. Kalmenson. *Positivity Bias,* 123.

Chapter 11

1. Stahl, James E., et al. 2015. "Relaxation Response and Resiliency Training and Its Effect on Healthcare Resource Utilization." *PLoS One* 10, no. 10: e0140212. https://doi.org/10.1371/journal.pone.0140212.

2. Park, Elyse R., et al. 2021. "A Comprehensive Resiliency Framework: Theoretical Model, Treatment, and Evaluation." *Global Advances in Health and Medicine* (March 24, 2021). https://doi.org/10.1177/21649561211000306.

3. Niharika, Lakshmi, et al. 2024. "The Mind-Body Connection in Stress and Immunity: A Systematic Review." *European Journal of Healthcare Bulletin* 14, no. 6: 303–306. https://www.healthcare-

bulletin.co.uk/article/the-mind-body-connection-in-stress-and-immunity-a-systematic-review-2577/.

4. Shields, G. S., et al. 2020. "Psychosocial Interventions and Immune System Function: A Systematic Review and Meta-Analysis of Randomized Clinical Trials." *JAMA Psychiatry* 77, no. 10: 1031–1043. doi:10.1001/jamapsychiatry.2020.0431.

5. American Psychological Association. 2011. "Building Your Resilience" (PDF). https://www.apaservices.org/practice/good-practice/building-resilience.pdf.

6. "Boosting Your Resilience / Strategies for Strengthening Resilience" (online course). Harvard Health Publishing. https://www.harvardhealthonlinelearning.com/learn/course/stress-management/boosting-your-resilience/strategies-for-strengthening-resilience?page=16.

7. Igros Kodesh. Vol. 7, p. 197: "Every descent and concealment is nothing but preparation for a greater elevation." Kehot Publication Society.

8. Likkutei Sichos. Vol. 15, p. 39: "The Rebbe elaborates on the principle that challenges are opportunities for growth." Chabad.org.

Chapter 12

1. Horton, Richard. 2015. "Offline: What is Medicine's 5 Sigma?" *The Lancet* 385 (April 11, 2015): 1380. http://www.thelancet.com/pdfs/journals/lancet/PIIS 0140-6736%2815%2960696-1.pdf.

2. Benson and Proctor. *Relaxation Revolution*, xiii.

3. Benson and Klipper. *Relaxation Response*, 4, 39.

4. Benson and Klipper. *Relaxation Response*, 160.

5. Benson and Proctor. *Relaxation Revolution*, 109–201.

6. Benson and Proctor. *Relaxation Revolution*, 16.

7. "The Science Behind Relaxation Response and Building Resilience: Our Research." n.d. The Benson-Henry Institute for Mind Body Medicine. https://bensonhenryinstitute.org/research-our-research/.

8. Benson and Proctor. *Relaxation Revolution*, 16.

9. Benson and Proctor. *Relaxation Revolution*, 15–16.

10. Benson and Proctor. *Relaxation Revolution*, 16.

11. Benson and Proctor. *Relaxation Revolution*, 60–70.

12. Benson and Proctor. *Relaxation Revolution*, 63–64.

13. Benson and Proctor. *Relaxation Revolution*, 64–66.

14. Benson and Proctor. *Relaxation Revolution*, 66.

15. Benson and Proctor. *Relaxation Revolution*, 66–68.

16. Benson and Proctor. *Relaxation Revolution*, 68.

17. Benson and Proctor. *Relaxation Revolution*, 68–69.

18. Benson and Proctor. *Relaxation Revolution*, 69.

19. Benson and Proctor. *Relaxation Revolution*, 69–70.

Chapter 13

1. Siegel, Aryeh. 2018. *Transcendental Deception.* Los Angeles: Janreg Press.

2. Hassan, Steven. n.d. "Bite Model of Authoritarian Control." Freedom of Mind Resource Center. https://freedomofmind.com/cult-mind-control/bite-model-pdf-download/#emotion.

Chapter 14

1. Yoga Alliance Foundation. 2016. "2016 Yoga in America Study Conducted by Yoga Journal and Yoga Alliance Reveals Growth and Benefits of the Practice" (press release: January 13, 2016). Yoga Alliance.

https://www.yogaalliance.org/Get_Involved/Media_Inquiries/2016_Yoga_in_America_Study_Conducted_by_Yoga_Journal_and_Yoga_Alliance_Reveals_Growth_and_Benefits_of_the_Practice.

2. Brodesser-Akner, Taffy. 2010. "Is Yoga Kosher?" Community section. *Tablet* (January 5, 2010). https://www.tabletmag.com/sections/community/articles/is-yoga-kosher.

3. See Appendix A, Letter 7 on yoga.

4. GalEinai, Imry. 2018. "Yoga: Can It Be Kosher? Rav Ginsburgh Addresses the Question." Inner.org. https://www.inner.org/chassidut/yoga-can-it-be-kosher-rav-ginsburgh-addresses-the-question.

5. Denbe, Shelly. 2014. *Wrestling with Yoga: Journey of a Jewish Soul.* Scotts Valley, California: CreateSpace, 26–29.

6. Denbe. Wrestling with Yoga, 31.

7. Denbe. Wrestling with Yoga, 31–32.

8. GalEinai. "Yoga: Can It Be Kosher?"

9. Denbe. Wrestling with Yoga, 35–36.

10. Machon Shmuel Institute. *Yoga, Can it be Kosher?*, 44–56.

11. Levi, Sarah. 2019. "Yoga and the Jews." *Jerusalem Post*. https://www.jpost.com/israel-news/yoga-and-the-jews-604443.

12. Gozlan, Audi. 2023. "Yoga Is Kosher?!" *Jewish Journal*. https://jewishjournal.com/commentary/356632/yoga-is-kosher/.

13. GalEinai. "Yoga: Can It Be Kosher?"

14. GalEinai. "Yoga: Can It Be Kosher?"

Chapter 15

1. Roth, Bob. 2022. *Strength in Stillness: The Power of Transcendental Meditation.* New York: Simon & Schuster, 32.

2. Excerpt from a speech given by Maharishi Mahesh Yogi, *Beacon Light of the Himalayas, 3 of 4* (n.d.). http://minet.org/www.trancenet.net/secrets/beacon/beacon1.shtml.

3. Roth. *Strength in Stillness*, 52.

4. Malnak v. Yogi, 440 F. Supp. 1284 (D.N.J. 1977). https://law.justia.com/cases/federal/district-courts/FSupp/440/1284/1817490/.

5. Benson and Klipper. *The Relaxation Response*.

Chapter 16

1. Brown, Candy. 2016. "Can 'Secular' Mindfulness Be Separated from Religion?" In *Handbook of Mindfulness: Culture, Context, and Social Engagement*, 1st ed., edited by Ronald E. Purser, David Forbes, and Adam Burke. New York: Springer, 78.

2. Kabat-Zinn, Jon. 1994. *Wherever You Go, There You Are: Mindfulness Meditation in Everyday Life*. New York: Hyperion, 4.

3. Brown. "Secular Mindfulness," 79.

Bibliography

Adini, B., et al. "Depression and Anxiety Rates Rise Significantly during COVID-19 Pandemic." Tel Aviv University News. 2020. https://english.tau.ac.il/news/depression-covid19.

American Psychological Association. "Building Your Resilience" (PDF), April 2011. https://www.apaservices.org/practice/good-practice/building-resilience.pdf.

American Psychological Association. "Stress in America: Concerned for the Future, Battered by Inflation." 2022. Retrieved from https://www.apa.org/news/press/releases/stress/2022/concerned-future-inflation.

"Anxiety Disorders - Facts & Statistics." Anxiety & Depression Society of America. Last modified 3 Chesvan 5783 (October 28, 2022). https://adaa.org/understanding-anxiety/facts-statistics.

Avey, Holly, Kenneth B. Matheny, Anna Robbins, and Terry A. Jacobson. "Health Care Providers' Training, Perceptions, and Practices Regarding Stress and Health Outcomes." *Journal of the National Medical Association*

95, no. 9 (September 2003). PMID: 14527051; PMCID: PMC2594476.

Beck, Aaron T., A. John Rush, Brian F. Shaw, and Gary Emery. *Cognitive Therapy of Depression.* New York: Guilford, 1974.

Benson, Herbert, John F. Beary, and Mark P. Carol. "The Relaxation Response." *Psychiatry* 37, no. 1 (February 1974): 37–46. https://doi.org/10.1080/00332747.1974.11023785.

Benson, Herbert and Richard Friedman. "Harnessing the Power of the Placebo Effect and Renaming It 'Remembered Wellness.'" *Annual Review of Medicine* 47 (1996). https://doi.org/10.1146/annurev.med.47.1.193; PMID: 8712773.

Benson, Herbert, and Miriam Z. Klipper. *The Relaxation Response.* New York: Quill, 2001.

Benson, Herbert and William Proctor. *The Breakout Principle: How to Activate the Natural Trigger That Maximizes Creativity, Athletic Performance, Productivity, and Personal Well-Being.* New York: Scribner, 2003.

———. *Relaxation Revolution: The Science and Genetics of Mind Body Healing.* New York: Scribner, 1979.

Benson, Herbert and Marg Stark. *Timeless Healing—The Power and Biology of Belief.* New York: Simon and Schuster, 1996.

Bhasin, Manoj K., Jeffery A. Dusek, Bei-Hung Chang, Marie G. Joseph, John W. Denninger, Gregory L. Fricchione, Herbert Benson, and Towia A. Libermann. "Relaxation Response Induces Temporal Transcriptome Changes in Energy Metabolism, Insulin Secretion And Inflammatory Pathways." *PLoS One* 8, no. 5 (May 1, 2013). https://doi.org/10.1371/journal.pone.0062817.

"Boosting Your Resilience / Strategies for Strengthening Resilience" (online course). Harvard Health Publishing. https://www.harvardhealthonlinelearning.com/learn/course/stress-management/boosting-your-resilience/strategies-for-strengthening-resilience?page=16.

Brodesser-Akner, Taffy. "Is Yoga Kosher?" Community section. *Tablet*, January 5, 2010. https://www.tabletmag.com/sections/community/articles/is-yoga-kosher.

Brown, Candy. "Can 'Secular' Mindfulness Be Separated from Religion?" https://doi.org/10.1007/978-3-319-44019-4_6. In *Handbook of Mindfulness: Culture, Context, and Social Engagement*, 1st ed., edited by Ronald E. Purser, David Forbes, and Adam Burke. New York: Springer, 2016.

Carrington, Patricia. *Learn To Meditate Manual*. www.patcarrington.com.

Dalfin, Chaim. *Conversations With the Rebbe, Menachem Mendel Schneerson*. Los Angeles: JEC Publishing Company, 1996.

Denbe, Shelly. *Wrestling with Yoga: Journey of a Jewish Soul*. Scotts Valley, California: CreateSpace, 2014.

Dusek, Jeffery A., Bei-Hung Chang, Jamil Zaki, Sara Lazar, Aaron Deykin, George B. Stefano, Ann L. Wohlhueter, Patricia L. Hibberd, and Herbert Benson. "Association Between Oxygen Consumption And Nitric Oxide Production During The Relaxation Response." *Medical Science Monitor* 12, no. 1 (January 2006). Epub December 19, 2005. PMD: 16369463.

Dusek, Jeffery A., Hasan H. Otu, Ann L. Wolhueter, Manoj Bhasin, Luiz F. Zerbini, Marie G. Joseph, Herbert Benson, and Towia A. Libermann. "Genomic Counter-Stress Changes Induced by the Relaxation Response." *PLoS One* 3, no. 7 (July 2, 2008). https://doi.org/10.1371/journal.pone. 0002576.

Freeman, Tzvi. "What Is Bitachon?" Building Blocks of Jewish Thought (online library, n.d.). https://www.chabad.org/library/article_cdo/aid/1405289/jewish/Bitachon.htm.

GalEinai, Imry. "Yoga: Can It Be Kosher? Rav Ginsburgh Addresses the Question." Inner.org, April 20, 2018. https://www.inner.org/chassidut/yoga-can-it-be-kosher-rav-ginsburgh-addresses-the-question.

Ghert-Zand, Renee. "October 7 and War Trauma Will Lead to At Least 30,000 New Cases of PTSD, Expert Says." *The Times of Israel*, 12 Adar I 5784 (February 21, 2024). https://www.timesofisrael.com/october-7-and-war-trauma-will-lead-to-at-least-30000-new-cases-of-ptsd-expert-says/?utm_source=pocket_saves.

Gozlan, Audi. "Yoga Is Kosher?!" *Jewish Journal*, March 2, 2023. https://jewishjournal.com/commentary/356632/yoga-is-kosher/.

Hecht, Esther. "Peace of Mind." *Jerusalem Post,* 13 Tammuz 5732 (23 January 1998).

Horton, Richard. "Offline: What is Medicine's 5 Sigma?" *The Lancet* 385 (April 11, 2015). http://www.thelancet.com/pdfs/journals/lancet/PIIS0140-6736%2815%2960696-1.pdf.

Ibn Pekuda, Rabbeinu Bachya. *Shaar Habitachon—the Gate of Trust*. New York: Kehot Publication Society & Chayenu, 2021. https://www.chabad.org/library/article_cdo/aid/5478224/jewish/Introduction-Part-1.htm#lt=primary

Kabat-Zinn, Jon. *Wherever You Go, There You Are: Mindfulness Meditation in Everyday Life*. New York: Hyperion, 1994.

Kalmenson, Mendel. *Positivity Bias - Practical Wisdom for Positive Living*. New York: Ezra Press, 2019.

Kissel, Pierre and Dominique Barrucand. *Placebos et Effet Placebo en Médecine*. Paris: Masson, 1964.

Landes, Yehoshua P. "The Inside Story Of The Founding Of Jewish Meditation." *B'Or Ha' Torah* 23 (2014).

Lazar, Sara W., Catherine E. Kerr, Rachel H. Wasserman, Jeremy R. Gray, Douglas N. Greve, Michael T. Treadway, Metta MacGarvey, Brian T. Quinn, Jeffery A. Dusek, Herbert Benson, Scott L. Rauch, Christopher I. Moore, and Bruce Fischl. "Meditation Experience Is Associated with Increased Cortical Thickness." *Neuroreport* 16, no. 17 (November 28, 2005). https://doi.org/10,1097/01.wnr.0000186598.66243.10.

Lembo, Anthony, John M. Kelley, Judy Nee, Sarah Ballou, Johanna Iturrino, Vivian Cheng, Vikram Rangan, Jesse Katon, William Hirsch, Irving Kirsch, Kathryn Hall, Roger B. Davis, and Ted J. Kaptchuk. "Open-Label Placebo vs. Double-Blind Placebo for Irritable Bowel Syndrome: A Randomized Clinical Trial." *Pain* 162, no. 9 (September 1, 2021). https://doi.org/10.1097/j.pain.0000000000002234.

Levi, Sarah. "Yoga and the Jews." *The Jerusalem Post*, October 12, 2019. https://www.jpost.com/israel-news/yoga-and-the-jews-60444313.

Levine, Glenn N., Richard A. Lange, C. Noel Bairey-Merz, Richard J. Davidson, Kenneth Jamerson, Puja K. Mehta, Erin D. Michos, Keith Norris, Indranill Basu Ray, Karen L. Saban, Tina Shah, Richard Stein, and Sidney C. Smith Jr. "Meditation And Cardiovascular Risk Reduction: A Scientific Statement From The American Heart Association." *Journal of the American Heart Association* 8, no. 2 (September 28, 2017).

https://www.ahajournals.org/doi/10.1161/JAHA.117.002218.

Likkutei Sichos, Vol. XXXVI, p. 336 "Kosher Meditation" (Disc 60, Program 237, sicha of 13 Tammuz 5739).

Machon Shmuel Institute. *Yoga, Can it be Kosher?* The Rohr Jewish Learning Institute, 2018.

Marks, Hedy. "Stress Symptoms." *Find Your Calm: Managing Stress & Anxiety* (blog). WebMD. Last reviewed 23 Tishrei 5784 (October 8, 2023). https://www.webmd.com/balance/stress-management/stress-symptoms-effects_of-stress-on-the-body.

Miller, Chaim. *Turning Judaism Outward: A Biography of the Rebbe, Menachem M. Schneerson.* New York: Kol Menachem, 2014.

Ophir, Natan. "The Lubavitcher Rebbe's Call for a Scientific Non-Hasidic Meditation." *B'or HaTorah* 22 (2013).

Park, Elyse R., Christina M. Luberto, Emma Chad-Friedman, Lara Traeger, Daniel L. Hall, Giselle K. Perez, Brett Goshe, Ana-Maria Vranceanu, Margaret Baim, John W. Denninger, Gregory Fricchione, Herbert Benson, and Suzanne C. Lechner. "A Comprehensive Resiliency Framework: Theoretical Model, Treatment, and Evaluation." *Global Advances in Health and Medicine* 10 (March 4, 2021).

https://doi.org/10.1177/21649561211000306. PMID: 34377598; PMCID: PMC8327002.

Rankin, Lissa. *Mind Over Medicine: Scientific Proof That You Can Heal Yourself*. Carlsbad, California: Hay House, 2020.

Reb Akiva. "The Lubavitcher Rebbe on Yoga." Mystical Paths, August 20, 2013. https://www.mpaths.com/2013/08/the-lubavitcher-rebbe-on-yoga.html?utm_source=pocket_saves.

Roth, Bob. *Strength in Stillness: The Power of Transcendental Meditation*. New York: Simon & Schuster, 2022.

Siegel, Bernie. *Love, Medicine & Miracles*. New York: Harper & Row, 1986.

Siegel, Aryeh. *Transcendental Deception*. Los Angeles: Janreg Press, 2018.

Solan, Matthew. "The Real Power of Placebos." *Staying Healthy* (blog). Harvard Health Publishing. https://www.health.harvard.edu/staying-healthy/the-real-power-of-placebos.

Stahl, James E., Michelle L. Dossett, A. Scott LaJoie, John W. Denninger, Darshan H. Mehta, Roberta Goldman, Gregory L. Fricchione, and Herbert Benson. *Relaxation Response and Resiliency Training and Its Effect on*

Healthcare Resource Utilization. PLoS One 10, no. 10 (2015). https://doi.org/10.1371/journal.pone.01402122.

Stefano, George B., Gregory L. Fricchione, Brian T. Slingsby, and Herbert Benson. "The Placebo Effect And Relaxation Response: Neural Processes and Their Coupling to Constitutive Nitric Oxide." *Brain Research Reviews* 35, no. 1 (March 2001). https://doi.org/10.1016/S0165-0173(00)00047-3.

"The Science Behind Relaxation Response and Building Resilience: Our Research." The Benson-Henry Institute for Mind Body Medicine (n.d.). https://bensonhenryinstitute.org/research-our-research/.

"Transcendental Meditation Movement." Wikipedia, last edited May 23, 2024. https://en.wikipedia.org/wiki/Transcendental_Meditation_movement.

Twerski, Rabbi Abraham. "Here's My Story." *Weekly Stories Regarding the Rebbe*, Ed. March 1, 2014. New York: Jewish Educational Media, 2014.

Wallace, Robert K., Herbert Benson, and Archie F. Wilson. "A Wakeful Hypometabolic Physiological State." *American Journal of Physiology* 221, no. 3 (September 1971).

Wineberg, Sholom B. *Healthy in Body, Mind and Spirit*. New York: Sichos in English, 2005.

Yoga Alliance Foundation. "2016 Yoga in America Study Conducted by Yoga Journal and Yoga Alliance Reveals Growth and Benefits of the Practice" (press release). Yoga Alliance, January 13, 2016. https://www.yogaalliance.org/Get_Involved/Media_Inquiries/2016_Yoga_in_America_Study_Conducted_by_Yoga_Journal_and_Yoga_Alliance_Reveals_Growth_and_Benefits_of_the_Practice.

Zalman, Rabbi Schneur. *Likkutei Amarim Tanya - Bilingual Edition*. New York: Kehot Publication Society, 1973.

www.ingramcontent.com/pod-product-compliance
Lightning Source LLC
LaVergne TN
LVHW020431070526
838199LV00025B/593/J